by Philip Larkin

poetry
THE NORTH SHIP
XX POEMS
THE FANTASY POETS NO. 21
THE LESS DECEIVED (The Marvell Press)
THE WHITSUN WEDDINGS
HIGH WINDOWS
COLLECTED POEMS 1938–83

SELECTED LETTERS OF PHILIP LARKIN 1940–85
(edited by Anthony Thwaite)

THE OXFORD BOOK OF TWENTIETH CENTURY ENGLISH VERSE (ed.)

fiction
JILL
A GIRL IN WINTER
TROUBLE AT WILLOW GABLES AND OTHER FICTIONS
(edited by James Booth)

non-fiction
ALL WHAT JAZZ: A Record Diary 1961–71
REQUIRED WRITING: Miscellaneous Pieces 1955–82
FURTHER REQUIREMENTS:
Interviews, Broadcasts, Statements and Reviews 1952–85
(edited by Anthony Thwaite)

COLLECTED POEMS

Collected Poems

Philip Larkin

Edited and with an introduction

by Anthony Thwaite

Farrar, Straus and Giroux

New York

Farrar, Straus and Giroux
19 Union Square West, New York 10003

Library of Congress Cataloging-in-Publication Data
Larkin, Philip.
   [Poems]
   Collected poems / Philip Larkin ; edited and with an introduction
by Anthony Thwaite.— 1st American ed.
      p.   cm.
   Includes index.
   ISBN 0-374-52920-5 (pbk. : alk. paper)
   I. Thwaite, Anthony.   II. Title.

PR6023.A66A17 2004
821'.914—dc22

                                                            2003060846

www.fsgbooks.com

3   5   7   9   10   8   6   4   2

Contents

THE NORTH SHIP

THE LESS DECEIVED

THE WHITSUN WEDDINGS

HIGH WINDOWS

APPENDIX I: Uncollected Poems 1940–1972

APPENDIX II: Uncollected Poems 1974–1984

APPENDIX III: Composition Dates and
Dates of First Appearance

Introduction

When I began work on Philip Larkin's *Collected Poems*, a few months after his death in December 1985, I quickly became fascinated by the way in which he almost always carefully recorded the dates of composition in his manuscript notebooks, consistently from the autumn of 1944. Both published and unpublished poems were with few exceptions meticulously dated, and this fact made me decide (with the agreement of my fellow literary executors, Monica Jones and Andrew Motion) to make a chronological ordering of the 'mature' poems, to form the main part of the book, followed by juvenilia, also in chronological order. The first section included some obvious false starts and divagations, and the second included all the poems in the 1945 *The North Ship*, which Larkin had agreed to reissue in the 1966 Faber and Faber edition, however reluctantly, as a book in its own right.

The resulting edition of the *Collected Poems*, published in 1988, showed the growth of a major poet, testing, filtering, rejecting, modulating, achieving. It included a number of poems that do not appear here. Among them are 'An April Sunday', the unfinished 'The Dance', and 'Love Again' – poems which are among Larkin's most striking and memorable, but which he chose not to publish.

This new edition of Philip Larkin's poems is partly a considered response to suggestions that what was needed, too, was a book that followed Larkin's own deliberate ordering of his poems in each successive book ('I treat them like a music-hall bill: you know, contrast, difference in length, the comic, the Irish tenor, bring on the girls'), with perhaps an appendix taking in earlier published strays and also a handful of poems after *High Windows* had gone to press.

The present edition follows Larkin's own running order in *The North Ship*, *The Less Deceived*, *The Whitsun Weddings* and *High Windows*; and there are appendices of poems Larkin published in other places, beginning with some teenage poems (including his first *Listener* poem, in 1940). These poems include some which Larkin had collected in the pamphlet *XX Poems*, privately printed for him in Belfast in 1951. Though he selected most of them for *The Less Deceived* in 1955, he chose not to reprint several there. I do not include the poems which first appeared in his school magazine, *The Coventrian*. In a further appendix, I list both the final composition date and the first appearance of each poem. Those who would like to know more about the dates and whereabouts of Larkin's manuscripts are directed towards the apparatus in the *Collected Poems* (paperback, 1990), p. xxvii.

Anthony Thwaite

Acknowledgements

I am glad to pay tribute here to Barry Bloomfield, whose bibliography of Larkin, published by Faber in 1979, was a constant help, with this edition as with its precursor. Its revised and expanded version, published by the British Library and Oak Knoll Press in June 2002, appeared – sadly – soon after Barry's death: he had passed a final set of proofs.

As before, in the 1988 and 1990 *Collected Poems*, I must acknowledge the help, co-operation and advice of several people: Paul Keegan at Faber for initiating this edition; my fellow literary executor, Andrew Motion; Alistair Elliot; Peter Porter; Ann Thwaite. In addition, I would like to thank the enthusiasts of the Philip Larkin Society, especially James Booth, Maeve Brennan, Eddie Dawes, Jean Hartley, Don Lee and John Osborne.

A.T.

THE NORTH SHIP

July 1945

I

to Bruce Montgomery

All catches alight
At the spread of spring:
Birds crazed with flight
Branches that fling
Leaves up to the light –
Every one thing,
Shape, colour and voice,
Cries out, Rejoice!
    A drum taps: a wintry drum.

Gull, grass and girl
In air, earth and bed
Join the long whirl
Of all the resurrected,
Gather up and hurl
Far out beyond the dead
What life they can control –
All runs back to the whole.
    A drum taps: a wintry drum.

What beasts now hesitate
Clothed in cloudless air,
In whom desire stands straight?
What ploughman halts his pair
To kick a broken plate
Or coin turned up by the share?
What lovers worry much
That a ghost bids them touch?
    A drum taps: a wintry drum.

Let the wheel spin out,
Till all created things
With shout and answering shout

[3]

Cast off rememberings;
Let it all come about
Till centuries of springs
And all their buried men
Stand on the earth again.
    A drum taps: a wintry drum.

This was your place of birth, this daytime palace,
This miracle of glass, whose every hall
The light as music fills, and on your face
Shines petal-soft; sunbeams are prodigal
To show you pausing at a picture's edge
To puzzle out the name, or with a hand
Resting a second on a random page –

The clouds cast moving shadows on the land.

Are you prepared for what the night will bring?
The stranger who will never show his face,
But asks admittance; will you greet your doom
As final; set him loaves and wine; knowing
The game is finished when he plays his ace,
And overturn the table and go into the next room?

III

The moon is full tonight
And hurts the eyes,
It is so definite and bright.
What if it has drawn up
All quietness and certitude of worth
Wherewith to fill its cup,
Or mint a second moon, a paradise? –
For they are gone from earth.

Dawn

To wake, and hear a cock
Out of the distance crying,
To pull the curtains back
And see the clouds flying –
How strange it is
For the heart to be loveless, and as cold as these.

Conscript
for James Ballard Sutton

The ego's county he inherited
From those who tended it like farmers; had
All knowledge that the study merited,
The requisite contempt of good and bad;

But one Spring day his land was violated;
A bunch of horsemen curtly asked his name,
Their leader in a different dialect stated
A war was on for which he was to blame,

And he must help them. The assent he gave
Was founded on desire for self-effacement
In order not to lose his birthright; brave,
For nothing would be easier than replacement,

Which would not give him time to follow further
The details of his own defeat and murder.

VI

Kick up the fire, and let the flames break loose
To drive the shadows back;
Prolong the talk on this or that excuse,
Till the night comes to rest
While some high bell is beating two o'clock.
Yet when the guest
Has stepped into the windy street, and gone,
Who can confront
The instantaneous grief of being alone?
Or watch the sad increase
Across the mind of this prolific plant,
Dumb idleness?

VII

The horns of the morning
Are blowing, are shining,
The meadows are bright
  With the coldest dew;
The dawn reassembles.
Like the clash of gold cymbals
The sky spreads its vans out
  The sun hangs in view.

Here, where no love is,
All that was hopeless
And kept me from sleeping
  Is frail and unsure;
For never so brilliant,
Neither so silent
Nor so unearthly, has
  Earth grown before.

Winter

In the field, two horses,
Two swans on the river,
While a wind blows over
A waste of thistles
Crowded like men;
And now again
My thoughts are children
With uneasy faces
That awake and rise
Beneath running skies
From buried places.

For the line of a swan
Diagonal on water
Is the cold of winter,
And each horse like a passion
Long since defeated
Lowers its head,
And oh, they invade
My cloaked-up mind
Till memory unlooses
Its brooch of faces –
Streams far behind.

Then the whole heath whistles
In the leaping wind,
And shrivelled men stand
Crowding like thistles
To one fruitless place;
Yet still the miracles
Exhume in each face
Strong silken seed,

That to the static
Gold winter sun throws back
Endless and cloudless pride.

Climbing the hill within the deafening wind
The blood unfurled itself, was proudly borne
High over meadows where white horses stood;
Up the steep woods it echoed like a horn
Till at the summit under shining trees
It cried: Submission is the only good;
Let me become an instrument sharply stringed
For all things to strike music as they please.

How to recall such music, when the street
Darkens? Among the rain and stone places
I find only an ancient sadness falling,
Only hurrying and troubled faces,
The walking of girls' vulnerable feet,
The heart in its own endless silence kneeling.

X

Within the dream you said:
Let us kiss then,
In this room, in this bed,
But when all's done
We must not meet again.

Hearing this last word,
There was no lambing-night,
No gale-driven bird
Nor frost-encircled root
As cold as my heart.

Night-Music

At one the wind rose,
And with it the noise
Of the black poplars.

Long since had the living
By a thin twine
Been led into their dreams
Where lanterns shine
Under a still veil
Of falling streams;
Long since had the dead
Become untroubled
In the light soil.
There were no mouths
To drink of the wind,
Nor any eyes
To sharpen on the stars'
Wide heaven-holding,
Only the sound
Long sibilant-muscled trees
Were lifting up, the black poplars.

And in their blazing solitude
The stars sang in their sockets through the night:
'Blow bright, blow bright
The coal of this unquickened world.'

XII

Like the train's beat
Swift language flutters the lips
Of the Polish airgirl in the corner seat.
The swinging and narrowing sun
Lights her eyelashes, shapes
Her sharp vivacity of bone.
Hair, wild and controlled, runs back:
And gestures like these English oaks
Flash past the windows of her foreign talk.

The train runs on through wilderness
Of cities. Still the hammered miles
Diversify behind her face.
And all humanity of interest
Before her angled beauty falls,
As whorling notes are pressed
In a bird's throat, issuing meaningless
Through written skies; a voice
Watering a stony place.

XIII

I put my mouth
Close to running water:
Flow north, flow south,
It will not matter,
It is not love you will find.

I told the wind:
It took away my words:
It is not love you will find,
Only the bright-tongued birds,
Only a moon with no home.

It is not love you will find:
You have no limbs
Crying for stillness, you have no mind
Trembling with seraphim,
You have no death to come.

Nursery Tale

All I remember is
The horseman, the moonlit hedges,
The hoofbeats shut suddenly in the yard,
The hand finding the door unbarred:
And I recall the room where he was brought,
Hung black and candlelit; a sort
Of meal laid out in mockery; for though
His place was set, there was no more
Than one unpolished pewter dish, that bore
The battered carcase of a carrion crow.

So every journey that I make
Leads me, as in the story he was led,
To some new ambush, to some fresh mistake:
So every journey I begin foretells
A weariness of daybreak, spread
With carrion kisses, carrion farewells.

The Dancer

Butterfly
Or falling leaf,
Which ought I to imitate
In my dancing?

And if she were to admit
The world weaved by her feet
Is leafless, is incomplete?
And if she abandoned it,
Broke the pivoted dance,
Set loose the audience?
Then would the moon go raving,
The moon, the anchorless
Moon go swerving
Down at the earth for a catastrophic kiss.

The bottle is drunk out by one;
At two, the book is shut;
At three, the lovers lie apart,
Love and its commerce done;
And now the luminous watch-hands
Show after four o'clock,
Time of night when straying winds
Trouble the dark.

And I am sick for want of sleep;
So sick, that I can half-believe
The soundless river pouring from the cave
Is neither strong, nor deep;
Only an image fancied in conceit.
I lie and wait for morning, and the birds,
The first steps going down the unswept street,
Voices of girls with scarves around their heads.

XVII

To write one song, I said,
As sad as the sad wind
That walks around my bed,
Having one simple fall
As a candle-flame swells, and is thinned,
As a curtain stirs by the wall
– For this I must visit the dead.
Headstone and wet cross,
Paths where the mourners tread,
A solitary bird,
These call up the shade of loss,
Shape word to word.

That stones would shine like gold
Above each sodden grave,
This, I had not foretold,
Nor the birds' clamour, nor
The image morning gave
Of more and ever more,
As some vast seven-piled wave,
Mane-flinging, manifold,
Streams at an endless shore.

XVIII

If grief could burn out
Like a sunken coal,
The heart would rest quiet,
The unrent soul
Be still as a veil;
But I have watched all night

The fire grow silent,
The grey ash soft:
And I stir the stubborn flint
The flames have left,
And grief stirs, and the deft
Heart lies impotent.

XIX

Ugly Sister

I will climb thirty steps to my room,
Lie on my bed;
Let the music, the violin, cornet and drum
Drowse from my head.

Since I was not bewitched in adolescence
And brought to love,
I will attend to the trees and their gracious silence,
To winds that move.

I see a girl dragged by the wrists
Across a dazzling field of snow,
And there is nothing in me that resists.
Once it would not be so;
Once I should choke with powerless jealousies;
But now I seem devoid of subtlety,
As simple as the things I see,
Being no more, no less, than two weak eyes.

There is snow everywhere,
Snow in one blinding light.
Even snow smudged in her hair
As she laughs and struggles, and pretends to fight;
And still I have no regret;
Nothing so wild, nothing so glad as she
Rears up in me,
And would not, though I watched an hour yet.

So I walk on. Perhaps what I desired
– That long and sickly hope, someday to be
As she is – gave a flicker and expired;
For the first time I'm content to see
What poor mortar and bricks
I have to build with, knowing that I can
Never in seventy years be more a man
Than now – a sack of meal upon two sticks.

So I walk on. And yet the first brick's laid.
Else how should two old ragged men
Clearing the drifts with shovels and a spade
Bring up my mind to fever-pitch again?
How should they sweep the girl clean from my heart,
With no more done

Than to stand coughing in the sun,
Then stoop and shovel snow onto a cart?

The beauty dries my throat.
Now they express
All that's content to wear a worn-out coat,
All actions done in patient hopelessness,
All that ignores the silences of death,
Thinking no further than the hand can hold,
All that grows old,
Yet works on uselessly with shortened breath.

Damn all explanatory rhymes!
To be that girl! – but that's impossible;
For me the task's to learn the many times
When I must stoop, and throw a shovelful:
I must repeat until I live the fact
That everything's remade
With shovel and spade;
That each dull day and each despairing act

Builds up the crags from which the spirit leaps
– The beast most innocent
That is so fabulous it never sleeps;
If I can keep against all argument
Such image of a snow-white unicorn,
Then as I pray it may for sanctuary
Descend at last to me,
And put into my hand its golden horn.

I dreamed of an out-thrust arm of land
Where gulls blew over a wave
That fell along miles of sand;
And the wind climbed up the caves
To tear at a dark-faced garden
Whose black flowers were dead,
And broke round a house we slept in,
A drawn blind and a bed.

I was sleeping, and you woke me
To walk on the chilled shore
Of a night with no memory,
Till your voice forsook my ear
Till your two hands withdrew
And I was empty of tears,
On the edge of a bricked and streeted sea
And a cold hill of stars.

XXII

One man walking a deserted platform;
Dawn coming, and rain
Driving across a darkening autumn;
One man restlessly waiting a train
While round the streets the wind runs wild,
Beating each shuttered house, that seems
Folded full of the dark silk of dreams,
A shell of sleep cradling a wife or child.

Who can this ambition trace,
To be each dawn perpetually journeying?
To trick this hour when lovers re-embrace
With the unguessed-at heart riding
The winds as gulls do? What lips said
Starset and cockcrow call the dispossessed
On to the next desert, lest
Love sink a grave round the still-sleeping head?

XXIII

If hands could free you, heart,
   Where would you fly?
Far, beyond every part
Of earth this running sky
Makes desolate? Would you cross
City and hill and sea,
   If hands could set you free?

I would not lift the latch;
   For I could run
Through fields, pit-valleys, catch
All beauty under the sun –
Still end in loss:
I should find no bent arm, no bed
   To rest my head.

Love, we must part now: do not let it be
Calamitous and bitter. In the past
There has been too much moonlight and self-pity:
Let us have done with it: for now at last
Never has sun more boldly paced the sky,
Never were hearts more eager to be free,
To kick down worlds, lash forests; you and I
No longer hold them; we are husks, that see
The grain going forward to a different use.

There is regret. Always, there is regret.
But it is better that our lives unloose,
As two tall ships, wind-mastered, wet with light,
Break from an estuary with their courses set,
And waving part, and waving drop from sight.

Morning has spread again
Through every street,
And we are strange again;
For should we meet
How can I tell you that
Last night you came
Unbidden, in a dream?
And how forget
That we had worn down love good-humouredly,
Talking in fits and starts
As friends, as they will be
Who have let passion die within their hearts.
Now, watching the red east expand,
I wonder love can have already set
In dreams, when we've not met
More times than I can number on one hand.

XXVI

This is the first thing
I have understood:
Time is the echo of an axe
Within a wood.

XXVII

Heaviest of flowers, the head
Forever hangs above a stormless bed;
Hands that the heart can govern
Shall be at last by darker hands unwoven;
Every exultant sense
Unstrung to silence –
The sun drift away.

And all the memories that best
Run back beyond this season of unrest
Shall lie upon the earth
That gave them birth.
Like fallen apples, they will lose
Their sweetness at the bruise,
And then decay.

XXVIII

Is it for now or for always,
The world hangs on a stalk?
Is it a trick or a trysting-place,
The woods we have found to walk?

Is it a mirage or miracle,
Your lips that lift at mine:
And the suns like a juggler's juggling-balls,
Are they a sham or a sign?

Shine out, my sudden angel,
Break fear with breast and brow,
I take you now and for always,
For always is always now.

XXIX

Pour away that youth
That overflows the heart
Into hair and mouth;
Take the grave's part,
Tell the bone's truth.

Throw away that youth
That jewel in the head
That bronze in the breath;
Walk with the dead
For fear of death.

So through that unripe day you bore your head,
And the day was plucked and tasted bitter,
As if still cold among the leaves. Instead,
It was your severed image that grew sweeter,
That floated, wing-stiff, focused in the sun
Along uncertainty and gales of shame
Blown out before I slept. Now you are one
I dare not think alive: only a name
That chimes occasionally, as a belief
Long since embedded in the static past.

Summer broke and drained. Now we are safe.
The days lose confidence, and can be faced
Indoors. This is your last, meticulous hour,
Cut, gummed; pastime of a provincial winter.

The North Ship
Legend

I saw three ships go sailing by,
Over the sea, the lifting sea,
And the wind rose in the morning sky,
And one was rigged for a long journey.

The first ship turned towards the west,
Over the sea, the running sea,
And by the wind was all possessed
And carried to a rich country.

The second turned towards the east,
Over the sea, the quaking sea,
And the wind hunted it like a beast
To anchor in captivity.

The third ship drove towards the north,
Over the sea, the darkening sea,
But no breath of wind came forth,
And the decks shone frostily.

The northern sky rose high and black
Over the proud unfruitful sea,
East and west the ships came back
Happily or unhappily:

But the third went wide and far
Into an unforgiving sea
Under a fire-spilling star,
And it was rigged for a long journey.

Songs
65° N

My sleep is made cold
By a recurrent dream
Where all things seem
Sickeningly to poise
On emptiness, on stars
Drifting under the world.

When waves fling loudly
And fall at the stern,
I am wakened each dawn
Increasingly to fear
Sail-stiffening air,
The birdless sea.

Light strikes from the ice:
Like one who near death
Savours the serene breath,
I grow afraid,
Now the bargain is made,
That dream draws close.

70° N
Fortunetelling

'You will go a long journey,
In a strange bed take rest,
And a dark girl will kiss you
As softly as the breast
Of an evening bird comes down
Covering its own nest.

'She will cover your mouth
Lest memory exclaim
At her bending face,
Knowing it is the same
As one who long since died
Under a different name.'

75° N
Blizzard

Suddenly clouds of snow
Begin assaulting the air,
As falling, as tangled
As a girl's thick hair.

Some see a flock of swans,
Some a fleet of ships
Or a spread winding-sheet,
But the snow touches my lips

And beyond all doubt I know
A girl is standing there
Who will take no lovers
Till she winds me in her hair.

[38]

Above 80° N

'A woman has ten claws,'
Sang the drunken boatswain;
Farther than Betelgeuse,
More brilliant than Orion
Or the planets Venus and Mars,
The star flames on the ocean;
'A woman has ten claws,'
Sang the drunken boatswain.

Waiting for breakfast, while she brushed her hair,
I looked down at the empty hotel yard
Once meant for coaches. Cobblestones were wet,
But sent no light back to the loaded sky,
Sunk as it was with mist down to the roofs.
Drainpipes and fire-escape climbed up
Past rooms still burning their electric light:
I thought: Featureless morning, featureless night.

Misjudgment: for the stones slept, and the mist
Wandered absolvingly past all it touched,
Yet hung like a stayed breath; the lights burnt on,
Pin-points of undisturbed excitement; beyond the glass
The colourless vial of day painlessly spilled
My world back after a year, my lost lost world
Like a cropping deer strayed near my path again,
Bewaring the mind's least clutch. Turning, I kissed her,
Easily for sheer joy tipping the balance to love.

But, tender visiting,
Fallow as a deer or an unforced field,
How would you have me? Towards your grace
My promises meet and lock and race like rivers,
But only when you choose. Are you jealous of her?
Will you refuse to come till I have sent
Her terribly away, importantly live
Part invalid, part baby, and part saint?

THE LESS DECEIVED

November 1955

Lines on a Young Lady's Photograph Album

At last you yielded up the album, which,
Once open, sent me distracted. All your ages
Matt and glossy on the thick black pages!
Too much confectionery, too rich:
I choke on such nutritious images.

My swivel eye hungers from pose to pose –
In pigtails, clutching a reluctant cat;
Or furred yourself, a sweet girl-graduate;
Or lifting a heavy-headed rose
Beneath a trellis, or in a trilby hat

(Faintly disturbing, that, in several ways) –
From every side you strike at my control,
Not least through these disquieting chaps who loll
At ease about your earlier days:
Not quite your class, I'd say, dear, on the whole.

But o, photography! as no art is,
Faithful and disappointing! that records
Dull days as dull, and hold-it smiles as frauds,
And will not censor blemishes
Like washing-lines, and Hall's-Distemper boards,

But shows the cat as disinclined, and shades
A chin as doubled when it is, what grace
Your candour thus confers upon her face!
How overwhelmingly persuades
That this is a real girl in a real place,

In every sense empirically true!
Or is it just *the past*? Those flowers, that gate,
These misty parks and motors, lacerate

Simply by being over; you
Contract my heart by looking out of date.

Yes, true; but in the end, surely, we cry
Not only at exclusion, but because
It leaves us free to cry. We know *what was*
Won't call on us to justify
Our grief, however hard we yowl across

The gap from eye to page. So I am left
To mourn (without a chance of consequence)
You, balanced on a bike against a fence;
To wonder if you'd spot the theft
Of this one of you bathing; to condense,

In short, a past that no one now can share,
No matter whose your future; calm and dry,
It holds you like a heaven, and you lie
Unvariably lovely there,
Smaller and clearer as the years go by.

Wedding-Wind

The wind blew all my wedding-day,
And my wedding-night was the night of the high wind;
And a stable door was banging, again and again,
That he must go and shut it, leaving me
Stupid in candlelight, hearing rain,
Seeing my face in the twisted candlestick,
Yet seeing nothing. When he came back
He said the horses were restless, and I was sad
That any man or beast that night should lack
The happiness I had.

                Now in the day
All's ravelled under the sun by the wind's blowing.
He has gone to look at the floods, and I
Carry a chipped pail to the chicken-run,
Set it down, and stare. All is the wind
Hunting through clouds and forests, thrashing
My apron and the hanging cloths on the line.
Can it be borne, this bodying-forth by wind
Of joy my actions turn on, like a thread
Carrying beads? Shall I be let to sleep
Now this perpetual morning shares my bed?
Can even death dry up
These new delighted lakes, conclude
Our kneeling as cattle by all-generous waters?

Places, Loved Ones

No, I have never found
The place where I could say
This is my proper ground,
Here I shall stay;
Nor met that special one
Who has an instant claim
On everything I own
Down to my name;

To find such seems to prove
You want no choice in where
To build, or whom to love;
You ask them to bear
You off irrevocably,
So that it's not your fault
Should the town turn dreary,
The girl a dolt.

Yet, having missed them, you're
Bound, none the less, to act
As if what you settled for
Mashed you, in fact;
And wiser to keep away
From thinking you still might trace
Uncalled-for to this day
Your person, your place.

Coming

On longer evenings,
Light, chill and yellow,
Bathes the serene
Foreheads of houses.
A thrush sings,
Laurel-surrounded
In the deep bare garden,
Its fresh-peeled voice
Astonishing the brickwork.
It will be spring soon,
It will be spring soon –
And I, whose childhood
Is a forgotten boredom,
Feel like a child
Who comes on a scene
Of adult reconciling,
And can understand nothing
But the unusual laughter,
And starts to be happy.

Reasons for Attendance

The trumpet's voice, loud and authoritative,
Draws me a moment to the lighted glass
To watch the dancers – all under twenty-five –
Shifting intently, face to flushed face,
Solemnly on the beat of happiness.

– Or so I fancy, sensing the smoke and sweat,
The wonderful feel of girls. Why be out here?
But then, why be in there? Sex, yes, but what
Is sex? Surely, to think the lion's share
Of happiness is found by couples – sheer

Inaccuracy, as far as I'm concerned.
What calls me is that lifted, rough-tongued bell
(Art, if you like) whose individual sound
Insists I too am individual.
It speaks; I hear; others may hear as well,

But not for me, nor I for them; and so
With happiness. Therefore I stay outside,
Believing this; and they maul to and fro,
Believing that; and both are satisfied,
If no one has misjudged himself. Or lied.

Dry-Point

Endlessly, time-honoured irritant,
A bubble is restively forming at your tip.
Burst it as fast as we can –
It will grow again, until we begin dying.

Silently it inflates, till we're enclosed
And forced to start the struggle to get out:
Bestial, intent, real.
The wet spark comes, the bright blown walls collapse,

But what sad scapes we cannot turn from then:
What ashen hills! what salted, shrunken lakes!
How leaden the ring looks,
Birmingham magic all discredited,

And how remote that bare and sunscrubbed room,
Intensely far, that padlocked cube of light
We neither define nor prove,
Where you, we dream, obtain no right of entry.

Next, Please

Always too eager for the future, we
Pick up bad habits of expectancy.
Something is always approaching; every day
Till then we say,

Watching from a bluff the tiny, clear,
Sparkling armada of promises draw near.
How slow they are! And how much time they waste,
Refusing to make haste!

Yet still they leave us holding wretched stalks
Of disappointment, for, though nothing balks
Each big approach, leaning with brasswork prinked,
Each rope distinct,

Flagged, and the figurehead with golden tits
Arching our way, it never anchors; it's
No sooner present than it turns to past.
Right to the last

We think each one will heave to and unload
All good into our lives, all we are owed
For waiting so devoutly and so long.
But we are wrong:

Only one ship is seeking us, a black-
Sailed unfamiliar, towing at her back
A huge and birdless silence. In her wake
No waters breed or break.

Going

There is an evening coming in
Across the fields, one never seen before,
That lights no lamps.

Silken it seems at a distance, yet
When it is drawn up over the knees and breast
It brings no comfort.

Where has the tree gone, that locked
Earth to the sky? What is under my hands,
That I cannot feel?

What loads my hands down?

Wants

Beyond all this, the wish to be alone:
However the sky grows dark with invitation-cards
However we follow the printed directions of sex
However the family is photographed under the flagstaff –
Beyond all this, the wish to be alone.

Beneath it all, desire of oblivion runs:
Despite the artful tensions of the calendar,
The life insurance, the tabled fertility rites,
The costly aversion of the eyes from death –
Beneath it all, desire of oblivion runs.

Maiden Name

Marrying left your maiden name disused.
Its five light sounds no longer mean your face,
Your voice, and all your variants of grace;
For since you were so thankfully confused
By law with someone else, you cannot be
Semantically the same as that young beauty:
It was of her that these two words were used.

Now it's a phrase applicable to no one,
Lying just where you left it, scattered through
Old lists, old programmes, a school prize or two,
Packets of letters tied with tartan ribbon –
Then is it scentless, weightless, strengthless, wholly
Untruthful? Try whispering it slowly.
No, it means you. Or, since you're past and gone,

It means what we feel now about you then:
How beautiful you were, and near, and young,
So vivid, you might still be there among
Those first few days, unfingermarked again.
So your old name shelters our faithfulness,
Instead of losing shape and meaning less
With your depreciating luggage laden.

Born Yesterday
for Sally Amis

Tightly-folded bud,
I have wished you something
None of the others would:
Not the usual stuff
About being beautiful,
Or running off a spring
Of innocence and love –
They will all wish you that,
And should it prove possible,
Well, you're a lucky girl.

But if it shouldn't, then
May you be ordinary;
Have, like other women,
An average of talents:
Not ugly, not good-looking,
Nothing uncustomary
To pull you off your balance,
That, unworkable itself,
Stops all the rest from working.
In fact, may you be dull –
If that is what a skilled,
Vigilant, flexible,
Unemphasised, enthralled
Catching of happiness is called.

Whatever Happened?

At once whatever happened starts receding.
Panting, and back on board, we line the rail
With trousers ripped, light wallets, and lips bleeding.

Yes, gone, thank God! Remembering each detail
We toss for half the night, but find next day
All's kodak-distant. Easily, then (though pale),

'Perspective brings significance,' we say,
Unhooding our photometers, and, snap!
What can't be printed can be thrown away.

Later, it's just a latitude: the map
Points out how unavoidable it was:
'Such coastal bedding always means mishap.'

Curses? The dark? Struggling? Where's the source
Of these yarns now (except in nightmares, of course)?

No Road

Since we agreed to let the road between us
Fall to disuse,
And bricked our gates up, planted trees to screen us,
And turned all time's eroding agents loose,
Silence, and space, and strangers – our neglect
Has not had much effect.

Leaves drift unswept, perhaps; grass creeps unmown;
No other change.
So clear it stands, so little overgrown,
Walking that way tonight would not seem strange,
And still would be allowed. A little longer,
And time will be the stronger,

Drafting a world where no such road will run
From you to me;
To watch that world come up like a cold sun,
Rewarding others, is my liberty.
Not to prevent it is my will's fulfilment.
Willing it, my ailment.

Wires

The widest prairies have electric fences,
For though old cattle know they must not stray
Young steers are always scenting purer water
Not here but anywhere. Beyond the wires

Leads them to blunder up against the wires
Whose muscle-shredding violence gives no quarter.
Young steers become old cattle from that day,
Electric limits to their widest senses.

Church Going

Once I am sure there's nothing going on
I step inside, letting the door thud shut.
Another church: matting, seats, and stone,
And little books; sprawlings of flowers, cut
For Sunday, brownish now; some brass and stuff
Up at the holy end; the small neat organ;
And a tense, musty, unignorable silence,
Brewed God knows how long. Hatless, I take off
My cycle-clips in awkward reverence,

Move forward, run my hand around the font.
From where I stand, the roof looks almost new –
Cleaned, or restored? Someone would know: I don't.
Mounting the lectern, I peruse a few
Hectoring large-scale verses, and pronounce
'Here endeth' much more loudly than I'd meant.
The echoes snigger briefly. Back at the door
I sign the book, donate an Irish sixpence,
Reflect the place was not worth stopping for.

Yet stop I did: in fact I often do,
And always end much at a loss like this,
Wondering what to look for; wondering, too,
When churches fall completely out of use
What we shall turn them into, if we shall keep
A few cathedrals chronically on show,
Their parchment, plate and pyx in locked cases,
And let the rest rent-free to rain and sheep.
Shall we avoid them as unlucky places?

Or, after dark, will dubious women come
To make their children touch a particular stone;
Pick simples for a cancer; or on some
Advised night see walking a dead one?

Power of some sort or other will go on
In games, in riddles, seemingly at random;
But superstition, like belief, must die,
And what remains when disbelief has gone?
Grass, weedy pavement, brambles, buttress, sky,

A shape less recognisable each week,
A purpose more obscure. I wonder who
Will be the last, the very last, to seek
This place for what it was; one of the crew
That tap and jot and know what rood-lofts were?
Some ruin-bibber, randy for antique,
Or Christmas-addict, counting on a whiff
Of gown-and-bands and organ-pipes and myrrh?
Or will he be my representative,

Bored, uninformed, knowing the ghostly silt
Dispersed, yet tending to this cross of ground
Through suburb scrub because it held unspilt
So long and equably what since is found
Only in separation – marriage, and birth,
And death, and thoughts of these – for which was built
This special shell? For, though I've no idea
What this accoutred frowsty barn is worth,
It pleases me to stand in silence here;

A serious house on serious earth it is,
In whose blent air all our compulsions meet,
Are recognised, and robed as destinies.
And that much never can be obsolete,
Since someone will forever be surprising
A hunger in himself to be more serious,
And gravitating with it to this ground,
Which, he once heard, was proper to grow wise in,
If only that so many dead lie round.

[59]

Age

My age fallen away like white swaddling
Floats in the middle distance, becomes
An inhabited cloud. I bend closer, discern
A lighted tenement scuttling with voices.
O you tall game I tired myself with joining!
Now I wade through you like knee-level weeds,

And they attend me, dear translucent bergs:
Silence and space. By now so much has flown
From the nest here of my head that I needs must turn
To know what prints I leave, whether of feet,
Or spoor of pads, or a bird's adept splay.

Myxomatosis

Caught in the centre of a soundless field
While hot inexplicable hours go by
What trap is this? Where were its teeth concealed?
You seem to ask.
                    I make a sharp reply,
Then clean my stick. I'm glad I can't explain
Just in what jaws you were to suppurate:
You may have thought things would come right again
If you could only keep quite still and wait.

Toads

Why should I let the toad *work*
    Squat on my life?
Can't I use my wit as a pitchfork
    And drive the brute off?

Six days of the week it soils
    With its sickening poison –
Just for paying a few bills!
    That's out of proportion.

Lots of folk live on their wits:
    Lecturers, lispers,
Losels, loblolly-men, louts –
    They don't end as paupers;

Lots of folk live up lanes
    With fires in a bucket,
Eat windfalls and tinned sardines –
    They seem to like it.

Their nippers have got bare feet,
    Their unspeakable wives
Are skinny as whippets – and yet
    No one actually *starves*.

Ah, were I courageous enough
    To shout *Stuff your pension!*
But I know, all too well, that's the stuff
    That dreams are made on:

For something sufficiently toad-like
    Squats in me, too;
Its hunkers are heavy as hard luck,
    And cold as snow,

And will never allow me to blarney
    My way to getting
The fame and the girl and the money
    All at one sitting.

I don't say, one bodies the other
    One's spiritual truth;
But I do say it's hard to lose either,
    When you have both.

Poetry of Departures

Sometimes you hear, fifth-hand,
As epitaph:
He chucked up everything
And just cleared off,
And always the voice will sound
Certain you approve
This audacious, purifying,
Elemental move.

And they are right, I think.
We all hate home
And having to be there:
I detest my room,
Its specially-chosen junk,
The good books, the good bed,
And my life, in perfect order:
So to hear it said

He walked out on the whole crowd
Leaves me flushed and stirred,
Like *Then she undid her dress*
Or *Take that you bastard;*
Surely I can, if he did?
And that helps me stay
Sober and industrious.
But I'd go today,

Yes, swagger the nut-strewn roads,
Crouch in the fo'c'sle
Stubbly with goodness, if
It weren't so artificial,
Such a deliberate step backwards
To create an object:
Books; china; a life
Reprehensibly perfect.

[64]

Triple Time

This empty street, this sky to blandness scoured,
This air, a little indistinct with autumn
Like a reflection, constitute the present –
A time traditionally soured,
A time unrecommended by event.

But equally they make up something else:
This is the future furthest childhood saw
Between long houses, under travelling skies,
Heard in contending bells –
An air lambent with adult enterprise,

And on another day will be the past,
A valley cropped by fat neglected chances
That we insensately forbore to fleece.
On this we blame our last
Threadbare perspectives, seasonal decrease.

Spring

Green-shadowed people sit, or walk in rings,
Their children finger the awakened grass,
Calmly a cloud stands, calmly a bird sings,
And, flashing like a dangled looking-glass,
Sun lights the balls that bounce, the dogs that bark,
The branch-arrested mist of leaf, and me,
Threading my pursed-up way across the park,
An indigestible sterility.

Spring, of all seasons most gratuitous,
Is fold of untaught flower, is race of water,
Is earth's most multiple, excited daughter;

And those she has least use for see her best,
Their paths grown craven and circuitous,
Their visions mountain-clear, their needs immodest.

Deceptions

'Of course I was drugged, and so heavily I did not regain my consciousness till the next morning. I was horrified to discover that I had been ruined, and for some days I was inconsolable, and cried like a child to be killed or sent back to my aunt.' Mayhew, *London Labour and the London Poor*

Even so distant, I can taste the grief,
Bitter and sharp with stalks, he made you gulp.
The sun's occasional print, the brisk brief
Worry of wheels along the street outside
Where bridal London bows the other way,
And light, unanswerable and tall and wide,
Forbids the scar to heal, and drives
Shame out of hiding. All the unhurried day
Your mind lay open like a drawer of knives.

Slums, years, have buried you. I would not dare
Console you if I could. What can be said,
Except that suffering is exact, but where
Desire takes charge, readings will grow erratic?
For you would hardly care
That you were less deceived, out on that bed,
Than he was, stumbling up the breathless stair
To burst into fulfilment's desolate attic.

I Remember, I Remember

Coming up England by a different line
For once, early in the cold new year,
We stopped, and, watching men with number-plates
Sprint down the platform to familiar gates,
'Why, Coventry!' I exclaimed. 'I was born here.'

I leant far out, and squinnied for a sign
That this was still the town that had been 'mine'
So long, but found I wasn't even clear
Which side was which. From where those cycle-crates
Were standing, had we annually departed

For all those family hols? ... A whistle went:
Things moved. I sat back, staring at my boots.
'Was that,' my friend smiled, 'where you "have your roots"?'
No, only where my childhood was unspent,
I wanted to retort, just where I started:

By now I've got the whole place clearly charted.
Our garden, first: where I did not invent
Blinding theologies of flowers and fruits,
And wasn't spoken to by an old hat.
And here we have that splendid family

I never ran to when I got depressed,
The boys all biceps and the girls all chest,
Their comic Ford, their farm where I could be
'Really myself'. I'll show you, come to that,
The bracken where I never trembling sat,

Determined to go through with it; where she
Lay back, and 'all became a burning mist'.
And, in those offices, my doggerel

Was not set up in blunt ten-point, nor read
By a distinguished cousin of the mayor,

Who didn't call and tell my father *There*
Before us, had we the gift to see ahead –
'You look as if you wished the place in Hell,'
My friend said, 'judging from your face.' 'Oh well,
I suppose it's not the place's fault,' I said.

'Nothing, like something, happens anywhere.'

Absences

Rain patters on a sea that tilts and sighs.
Fast-running floors, collapsing into hollows,
Tower suddenly, spray-haired. Contrariwise,
A wave drops like a wall: another follows,
Wilting and scrambling, tirelessly at play
Where there are no ships and no shallows.

Above the sea, the yet more shoreless day,
Riddled by wind, trails lit-up galleries:
They shift to giant ribbing, sift away.

Such attics cleared of me! Such absences!

Latest Face

Latest face, so effortless
Your great arrival at my eyes,
No one standing near could guess
Your beauty had no home till then;
Precious vagrant, recognise
My look, and do not turn again.

Admirer and admired embrace
On a useless level, where
I contain your current grace,
You my judgment; yet to move
Into real untidy air
Brings no lasting attribute –
Bargains, suffering, and love,
Not this always-planned salute.

Lies grow dark around us: will
The statue of your beauty walk?
Must I wade behind it, till
Something's found – or is not found –
Far too late for turning back?
Or, if I will not shift my ground,
Is your power actual – can
Denial of you duck and run,
Stay out of sight and double round,
Leap from the sun with mask and brand
And murder and not understand?

If, My Darling

If my darling were once to decide
Not to stop at my eyes,
But to jump, like Alice, with floating skirt into my head,

She would find no tables and chairs,
No mahogany claw-footed sideboards,
No undisturbed embers;

The tantalus would not be filled, nor the fender-seat cosy,
Nor the shelves stuffed with small-printed books for the Sabbath,
Nor the butler bibulous, the housemaids lazy:

She would find herself looped with the creep of varying light,
Monkey-brown, fish-grey, a string of infected circles
Loitering like bullies, about to coagulate;

Delusions that shrink to the size of a woman's glove,
Then sicken inclusively outwards. She would also remark
The unwholesome floor, as it might be the skin of a grave,

From which ascends an adhesive sense of betrayal,
A Grecian statue kicked in the privates, money,
A swill-tub of finer feelings. But most of all

She'd be stopping her ears against the incessant recital
Intoned by reality, larded with technical terms,
Each one double-yolked with meaning and meaning's rebuttal:

For the skirl of that bulletin unpicks the world like a knot,
And to hear how the past is past and the future neuter
Might knock my darling off her unpriceable pivot.

Skin

Obedient daily dress,
You cannot always keep
That unfakable young surface.
You must learn your lines –
Anger, amusement, sleep;
Those few forbidding signs

Of the continuous coarse
Sand-laden wind, time;
You must thicken, work loose
Into an old bag
Carrying a soiled name.
Parch then; be roughened; sag;

And pardon me, that I
Could find, when you were new,
No brash festivity
To wear you at, such as
Clothes are entitled to
Till the fashion changes.

Arrivals, Departures

This town has docks where channel boats come sidling;
Tame water lanes, tall sheds, the traveller sees
(His bag of samples knocking at his knees),
And hears, still under slackened engines gliding,
His advent blurted to the morning shore.

And we, barely recalled from sleep there, sense
Arrivals lowing in a doleful distance –
Horny dilemmas at the gate once more.
Come and choose wrong, they cry, *come and choose wrong*;
And so we rise. At night again they sound,

Calling the traveller now, the outward bound:
O not for long, they cry, *O not for long* –
And we are nudged from comfort, never knowing
How safely we may disregard their blowing,
Or if, this night, happiness too is going.

At Grass

The eye can hardly pick them out
From the cold shade they shelter in,
Till wind distresses tail and mane;
Then one crops grass, and moves about
– The other seeming to look on –
And stands anonymous again.

Yet fifteen years ago, perhaps
Two dozen distances sufficed
To fable them: faint afternoons
Of Cups and Stakes and Handicaps,
Whereby their names were artificed
To inlay faded, classic Junes –

Silks at the start: against the sky
Numbers and parasols: outside,
Squadrons of empty cars, and heat,
And littered grass: then the long cry
Hanging unhushed till it subside
To stop-press columns on the street.

Do memories plague their ears like flies?
They shake their heads. Dusk brims the shadows.
Summer by summer all stole away,
The starting-gates, the crowds and cries –
All but the unmolesting meadows.
Almanacked, their names live; they

Have slipped their names, and stand at ease,
Or gallop for what must be joy,
And not a fieldglass sees them home,
Or curious stop-watch prophesies:
Only the groom, and the groom's boy,
With bridles in the evening come.

THE WHITSUN WEDDINGS

February 1964

Here

Swerving east, from rich industrial shadows
And traffic all night north; swerving through fields
Too thin and thistled to be called meadows,
And now and then a harsh-named halt, that shields
Workmen at dawn; swerving to solitude
Of skies and scarecrows, haystacks, hares and pheasants,
And the widening river's slow presence,
The piled gold clouds, the shining gull-marked mud,

Gathers to the surprise of a large town:
Here domes and statues, spires and cranes cluster
Beside grain-scattered streets, barge-crowded water,
And residents from raw estates, brought down
The dead straight miles by stealing flat-faced trolleys,
Push through plate-glass swing doors to their desires –
Cheap suits, red kitchen-ware, sharp shoes, iced lollies,
Electric mixers, toasters, washers, driers –

A cut-price crowd, urban yet simple, dwelling
Where only salesmen and relations come
Within a terminate and fishy-smelling
Pastoral of ships up streets, the slave museum,
Tattoo-shops, consulates, grim head-scarfed wives;
And out beyond its mortgaged half-built edges
Fast-shadowed wheat-fields, running high as hedges,
Isolate villages, where removed lives

Loneliness clarifies. Here silence stands
Like heat. Here leaves unnoticed thicken,
Hidden weeds flower, neglected waters quicken,
Luminously-peopled air ascends;
And past the poppies bluish neutral distance

Ends the land suddenly beyond a beach
Of shapes and shingle. Here is unfenced existence:
Facing the sun, untalkative, out of reach.

Mr Bleaney

'This was Mr Bleaney's room. He stayed
The whole time he was at the Bodies, till
They moved him.' Flowered curtains, thin and frayed,
Fall to within five inches of the sill,

Whose window shows a strip of building land,
Tussocky, littered. 'Mr Bleaney took
My bit of garden properly in hand.'
Bed, upright chair, sixty-watt bulb, no hook

Behind the door, no room for books or bags –
'I'll take it.' So it happens that I lie
Where Mr Bleaney lay, and stub my fags
On the same saucer-souvenir, and try

Stuffing my ears with cotton-wool, to drown
The jabbering set he egged her on to buy.
I know his habits – what time he came down,
His preference for sauce to gravy, why

He kept on plugging at the four aways –
Likewise their yearly frame: the Frinton folk
Who put him up for summer holidays,
And Christmas at his sister's house in Stoke.

But if he stood and watched the frigid wind
Tousling the clouds, lay on the fusty bed
Telling himself that this was home, and grinned,
And shivered, without shaking off the dread

That how we live measures our own nature,
And at his age having no more to show
Than one hired box should make him pretty sure
He warranted no better, I don't know.

Nothing To Be Said

For nations vague as weed,
For nomads among stones,
Small-statured cross-faced tribes
And cobble-close families
In mill-towns on dark mornings
Life is slow dying.

So are their separate ways
Of building, benediction,
Measuring love and money
Ways of slow dying.
The day spent hunting pig
Or holding a garden-party,

Hours giving evidence
Or birth, advance
On death equally slowly.
And saying so to some
Means nothing; others it leaves
Nothing to be said.

Love Songs in Age

She kept her songs, they took so little space,
    The covers pleased her:
One bleached from lying in a sunny place,
One marked in circles by a vase of water,
One mended, when a tidy fit had seized her,
    And coloured, by her daughter –
So they had waited, till in widowhood
She found them, looking for something else, and stood

Relearning how each frank submissive chord
    Had ushered in
Word after sprawling hyphenated word,
And the unfailing sense of being young
Spread out like a spring-woken tree, wherein
    That hidden freshness sung,
That certainty of time laid up in store
As when she played them first. But, even more,

The glare of that much-mentioned brilliance, love,
    Broke out, to show
Its bright incipience sailing above,
Still promising to solve, and satisfy,
And set unchangeably in order. So
    To pile them back, to cry,
Was hard, without lamely admitting how
It had not done so then, and could not now.

Naturally the Foundation will Bear Your Expenses

Hurrying to catch my Comet
  One dark November day,
Which soon would snatch me from it
  To the sunshine of Bombay,
I pondered pages Berkeley
  Not three weeks since had heard,
Perceiving Chatto darkly
  Through the mirror of the Third.

Crowds, colourless and careworn,
  Had made my taxi late,
Yet not till I was airborne
  Did I recall the date –
That day when Queen and Minister
  And Band of Guards and all
Still act their solemn-sinister
  Wreath-rubbish in Whitehall.

It used to make me throw up,
  These mawkish nursery games:
O when will England grow up?
  – But I outsoar the Thames,
And dwindle off down Auster
  To greet Professor Lal
(He once met Morgan Forster),
  My contact and my pal.

Broadcast

Giant whispering and coughing from
Vast Sunday-full and organ-frowned-on spaces
Precede a sudden scuttle on the drum,
'The Queen', and huge resettling. Then begins
A snivel on the violins:
I think of your face among all those faces,

Beautiful and devout before
Cascades of monumental slithering,
One of your gloves unnoticed on the floor
Beside those new, slightly-outmoded shoes.
Here it goes quickly dark. I lose
All but the outline of the still and withering

Leaves on half-emptied trees. Behind
The glowing wavebands, rabid storms of chording
By being distant overpower my mind
All the more shamelessly, their cut-off shout
Leaving me desperate to pick out
Your hands, tiny in all that air, applauding.

Faith Healing

Slowly the women file to where he stands
Upright in rimless glasses, silver hair,
Dark suit, white collar. Stewards tirelessly
Persuade them onwards to his voice and hands,
Within whose warm spring rain of loving care
Each dwells some twenty seconds. *Now, dear child,
What's wrong*, the deep American voice demands,
And, scarcely pausing, goes into a prayer
Directing God about this eye, that knee.
Their heads are clasped abruptly; then, exiled

Like losing thoughts, they go in silence; some
Sheepishly stray, not back into their lives
Just yet; but some stay stiff, twitching and loud
With deep hoarse tears, as if a kind of dumb
And idiot child within them still survives
To re-awake at kindness, thinking a voice
At last calls them alone, that hands have come
To lift and lighten; and such joy arrives
Their thick tongues blort, their eyes squeeze grief, a crowd
Of huge unheard answers jam and rejoice –

What's wrong! Moustached in flowered frocks they shake:
By now, all's wrong. In everyone there sleeps
A sense of life lived according to love.
To some it means the difference they could make
By loving others, but across most it sweeps
As all they might have done had they been loved.
That nothing cures. An immense slackening ache,
As when, thawing, the rigid landscape weeps,
Spreads slowly through them – that, and the voice above
Saying *Dear child*, and all time has disproved.

For Sidney Bechet

That note you hold, narrowing and rising, shakes
Like New Orleans reflected on the water,
And in all ears appropriate falsehood wakes,

Building for some a legendary Quarter
Of balconies, flower-baskets and quadrilles,
Everyone making love and going shares –

Oh, play that thing! Mute glorious Storyvilles
Others may license, grouping round their chairs
Sporting-house girls like circus tigers (priced

Far above rubies) to pretend their fads,
While scholars *manqués* nod around unnoticed
Wrapped up in personnels like old plaids.

On me your voice falls as they say love should,
Like an enormous yes. My Crescent City
Is where your speech alone is understood,

And greeted as the natural noise of good,
Scattering long-haired grief and scored pity.

Home is so Sad

Home is so sad. It stays as it was left,
Shaped to the comfort of the last to go
As if to win them back. Instead, bereft
Of anyone to please, it withers so,
Having no heart to put aside the theft

And turn again to what it started as,
A joyous shot at how things ought to be,
Long fallen wide. You can see how it was:
Look at the pictures and the cutlery.
The music in the piano stool. That vase.

Toads Revisited

Walking around in the park
Should feel better than work:
The lake, the sunshine,
The grass to lie on,

Blurred playground noises
Beyond black-stockinged nurses –
Not a bad place to be.
Yet it doesn't suit me,

Being one of the men
You meet of an afternoon:
Palsied old step-takers,
Hare-eyed clerks with the jitters,

Waxed-fleshed out-patients
Still vague from accidents,
And characters in long coats
Deep in the litter-baskets –

All dodging the toad work
By being stupid or weak.
Think of being them!
Hearing the hours chime,

Watching the bread delivered,
The sun by clouds covered,
The children going home;
Think of being them,

Turning over their failures
By some bed of lobelias,
Nowhere to go but indoors,
No friends but empty chairs –

No, give me my in-tray,
My loaf-haired secretary,
My shall-I-keep-the-call-in-Sir:
What else can I answer,

When the lights come on at four
At the end of another year?
Give me your arm, old toad;
Help me down Cemetery Road.

Water

If I were called in
To construct a religion
I should make use of water.

Going to church
Would entail a fording
To dry, different clothes;

My liturgy would employ
Images of sousing,
A furious devout drench,

And I should raise in the east
A glass of water
Where any-angled light
Would congregate endlessly.

The Whitsun Weddings

That Whitsun, I was late getting away:
    Not till about
One-twenty on the sunlit Saturday
Did my three-quarters-empty train pull out,
All windows down, all cushions hot, all sense
Of being in a hurry gone. We ran
Behind the backs of houses, crossed a street
Of blinding windscreens, smelt the fish-dock; thence
The river's level drifting breadth began,
Where sky and Lincolnshire and water meet.

All afternoon, through the tall heat that slept
    For miles inland,
A slow and stopping curve southwards we kept.
Wide farms went by, short-shadowed cattle, and
Canals with floatings of industrial froth;
A hothouse flashed uniquely: hedges dipped
And rose: and now and then a smell of grass
Displaced the reek of buttoned carriage-cloth
Until the next town, new and nondescript,
Approached with acres of dismantled cars.

At first, I didn't notice what a noise
    The weddings made
Each station that we stopped at: sun destroys
The interest of what's happening in the shade,
And down the long cool platforms whoops and skirls
I took for porters larking with the mails,
And went on reading. Once we started, though,
We passed them, grinning and pomaded, girls
In parodies of fashion, heels and veils,
All posed irresolutely, watching us go,

As if out on the end of an event
　　Waving goodbye
To something that survived it. Struck, I leant
More promptly out next time, more curiously,
And saw it all again in different terms:
The fathers with broad belts under their suits
And seamy foreheads; mothers loud and fat;
An uncle shouting smut; and then the perms,
The nylon gloves and jewellery-substitutes,
The lemons, mauves, and olive-ochres that

Marked off the girls unreally from the rest.
　　Yes, from cafés
And banquet-halls up yards, and bunting-dressed
Coach-party annexes, the wedding-days
Were coming to an end. All down the line
Fresh couples climbed aboard: the rest stood round;
The last confetti and advice were thrown,
And, as we moved, each face seemed to define
Just what it saw departing: children frowned
At something dull; fathers had never known

Success so huge and wholly farcical;
　　The women shared
The secret like a happy funeral;
While girls, gripping their handbags tighter, stared
At a religious wounding. Free at last,
And loaded with the sum of all they saw,
We hurried towards London, shuffling gouts of steam.
Now fields were building-plots, and poplars cast
Long shadows over major roads, and for
Some fifty minutes, that in time would seem

Just long enough to settle hats and say
　　I nearly died,
A dozen marriages got under way.

They watched the landscape, sitting side by side
– An Odeon went past, a cooling tower,
And someone running up to bowl – and none
Thought of the others they would never meet
Or how their lives would all contain this hour.
I thought of London spread out in the sun,
Its postal districts packed like squares of wheat:

There we were aimed. And as we raced across
    Bright knots of rail
Past standing Pullmans, walls of blackened moss
Came close, and it was nearly done, this frail
Travelling coincidence; and what it held
Stood ready to be loosed with all the power
That being changed can give. We slowed again,
And as the tightened brakes took hold, there swelled
A sense of falling, like an arrow-shower
Sent out of sight, somewhere becoming rain.

Self's the Man

Oh, no one can deny
That Arnold is less selfish than I.
He married a woman to stop her getting away
Now she's there all day,

And the money he gets for wasting his life on work
She takes as her perk
To pay for the kiddies' clobber and the drier
And the electric fire,

And when he finishes supper
Planning to have a read at the evening paper
It's *Put a screw in this wall* –
He has no time at all,

With the nippers to wheel round the houses
And the hall to paint in his old trousers
And that letter to her mother
Saying *Won't you come for the summer.*

To compare his life and mine
Makes me feel a swine:
Oh, no one can deny
That Arnold is less selfish than I.

But wait, not so fast:
Is there such a contrast?
He was out for his own ends
Not just pleasing his friends;

And if it was such a mistake
He still did it for his own sake,
Playing his own game.
So he and I are the same,

Only I'm a better hand
At knowing what I can stand
Without them sending a van –
Or I suppose I can.

Take One Home for the Kiddies

On shallow straw, in shadeless glass,
Huddled by empty bowls, they sleep:
No dark, no dam, no earth, no grass –
Mam, get us one of them to keep.

Living toys are something novel,
But it soon wears off somehow.
Fetch the shoebox, fetch the shovel –
Mam, we're playing funerals now.

Days

What are days for?
Days are where we live.
They come, they wake us
Time and time over.
They are to be happy in:
Where can we live but days?

Ah, solving that question
Brings the priest and the doctor
In their long coats
Running over the fields.

MCMXIV

Those long uneven lines
Standing as patiently
As if they were stretched outside
The Oval or Villa Park,
The crowns of hats, the sun
On moustached archaic faces
Grinning as if it were all
An August Bank Holiday lark;

And the shut shops, the bleached
Established names on the sunblinds,
The farthings and sovereigns,
And dark-clothed children at play
Called after kings and queens,
The tin advertisements
For cocoa and twist, and the pubs
Wide open all day;

And the countryside not caring:
The place-names all hazed over
With flowering grasses, and fields
Shadowing Domesday lines
Under wheat's restless silence;
The differently-dressed servants
With tiny rooms in huge houses,
The dust behind limousines;

Never such innocence,
Never before or since,
As changed itself to past
Without a word – the men
Leaving the gardens tidy,
The thousands of marriages
Lasting a little while longer:
Never such innocence again.

Talking in Bed

Talking in bed ought to be easiest,
Lying together there goes back so far,
An emblem of two people being honest.

Yet more and more time passes silently.
Outside, the wind's incomplete unrest
Builds and disperses clouds about the sky,

And dark towns heap up on the horizon.
None of this cares for us. Nothing shows why
At this unique distance from isolation

It becomes still more difficult to find
Words at once true and kind,
Or not untrue and not unkind.

The Large Cool Store

The large cool store selling cheap clothes
Set out in simple sizes plainly
(Knitwear, Summer Casuals, Hose,
In browns and greys, maroon and navy)
Conjures the weekday world of those

Who leave at dawn low terraced houses
Timed for factory, yard and site.
But past the heaps of shirts and trousers
Spread the stands of Modes For Night:
Machine-embroidered, thin as blouses,

Lemon, sapphire, moss-green, rose
Bri-Nylon Baby-Dolls and Shorties
Flounce in clusters. To suppose
They share that world, to think their sort is
Matched by something in it, shows

How separate and unearthly love is,
Or women are, or what they do,
Or in our young unreal wishes
Seem to be: synthetic, new,
And natureless in ecstasies.

A Study of Reading Habits

When getting my nose in a book
Cured most things short of school,
It was worth ruining my eyes
To know I could still keep cool,
And deal out the old right hook
To dirty dogs twice my size.

Later, with inch-thick specs,
Evil was just my lark:
Me and my cloak and fangs
Had ripping times in the dark.
The women I clubbed with sex!
I broke them up like meringues.

Don't read much now: the dude
Who lets the girl down before
The hero arrives, the chap
Who's yellow and keeps the store,
Seem far too familiar. Get stewed:
Books are a load of crap.

As Bad as a Mile

Watching the shied core
Striking the basket, skidding across the floor,
Shows less and less of luck, and more and more

Of failure spreading back up the arm
Earlier and earlier, the unraised hand calm,
The apple unbitten in the palm.

Ambulances

Closed like confessionals, they thread
Loud noons of cities, giving back
None of the glances they absorb.
Light glossy grey, arms on a plaque,
They come to rest at any kerb:
All streets in time are visited.

Then children strewn on steps or road,
Or women coming from the shops
Past smells of different dinners, see
A wild white face that overtops
Red stretcher-blankets momently
As it is carried in and stowed,

And sense the solving emptiness
That lies just under all we do,
And for a second get it whole,
So permanent and blank and true.
The fastened doors recede. *Poor soul*,
They whisper at their own distress;

For borne away in deadened air
May go the sudden shut of loss
Round something nearly at an end,
And what cohered in it across
The years, the unique random blend
Of families and fashions, there

At last begin to loosen. Far
From the exchange of love to lie
Unreachable inside a room
The traffic parts to let go by
Brings closer what is left to come,
And dulls to distance all we are.

The Importance of Elsewhere

Lonely in Ireland, since it was not home,
Strangeness made sense. The salt rebuff of speech,
Insisting so on difference, made me welcome:
Once that was recognised, we were in touch.

Their draughty streets, end-on to hills, the faint
Archaic smell of dockland, like a stable,
The herring-hawker's cry, dwindling, went
To prove me separate, not unworkable.

Living in England has no such excuse:
These are my customs and establishments
It would be much more serious to refuse.
Here no elsewhere underwrites my existence.

Sunny Prestatyn

Come To Sunny Prestatyn
Laughed the girl on the poster,
Kneeling up on the sand
In tautened white satin.
Behind her, a hunk of coast, a
Hotel with palms
Seemed to expand from her thighs and
Spread breast-lifting arms.

She was slapped up one day in March.
A couple of weeks, and her face
Was snaggle-toothed and boss-eyed;
Huge tits and a fissured crotch
Were scored well in, and the space
Between her legs held scrawls
That set her fairly astride
A tuberous cock and balls

Autographed *Titch Thomas*, while
Someone had used a knife
Or something to stab right through
The moustached lips of her smile.
She was too good for this life.
Very soon, a great transverse tear
Left only a hand and some blue.
Now *Fight Cancer* is there.

First Sight

Lambs that learn to walk in snow
When their bleating clouds the air
Meet a vast unwelcome, know
Nothing but a sunless glare.
Newly stumbling to and fro
All they find, outside the fold,
Is a wretched width of cold.

As they wait beside the ewe,
Her fleeces wetly caked, there lies
Hidden round them, waiting too,
Earth's immeasurable surprise.
They could not grasp it if they knew,
What so soon will wake and grow
Utterly unlike the snow.

Dockery and Son

'Dockery was junior to you,
Wasn't he?' said the Dean. 'His son's here now.'
Death-suited, visitant, I nod. 'And do
You keep in touch with –' Or remember how
Black-gowned, unbreakfasted, and still half-tight
We used to stand before that desk, to give
'Our version' of 'these incidents last night'?
I try the door of where I used to live:

Locked. The lawn spreads dazzlingly wide.
A known bell chimes. I catch my train, ignored.
Canal and clouds and colleges subside
Slowly from view. But Dockery, good Lord,
Anyone up today must have been born
In '43, when I was twenty-one.
If he was younger, did he get this son
At nineteen, twenty? Was he that withdrawn

High-collared public-schoolboy, sharing rooms
With Cartwright who was killed? Well, it just shows
How much ... How little ... Yawning, I suppose
I fell asleep, waking at the fumes
And furnace-glares of Sheffield, where I changed,
And ate an awful pie, and walked along
The platform to its end to see the ranged
Joining and parting lines reflect a strong

Unhindered moon. To have no son, no wife,
No house or land still seemed quite natural.
Only a numbness registered the shock
Of finding out how much had gone of life,
How widely from the others. Dockery, now:
Only nineteen, he must have taken stock

Of what he wanted, and been capable
Of ... No, that's not the difference: rather, how

Convinced he was he should be added to!
Why did he think adding meant increase?
To me it was dilution. Where do these
Innate assumptions come from? Not from what
We think truest, or most want to do:
Those warp tight-shut, like doors. They're more a style
Our lives bring with them: habit for a while,
Suddenly they harden into all we've got

And how we got it; looked back on, they rear
Like sand-clouds, thick and close, embodying
For Dockery a son, for me nothing,
Nothing with all a son's harsh patronage.
Life is first boredom, then fear.
Whether or not we use it, it goes,
And leaves what something hidden from us chose,
And age, and then the only end of age.

Ignorance

Strange to know nothing, never to be sure
Of what is true or right or real,
But forced to qualify *or so I feel*,
Or *Well, it does seem so:*
Someone must know.

Strange to be ignorant of the way things work:
Their skill at finding what they need,
Their sense of shape, and punctual spread of seed,
And willingness to change;
Yes, it is strange,

Even to wear such knowledge – for our flesh
Surrounds us with its own decisions –
And yet spend all our life on imprecisions,
That when we start to die
Have no idea why.

Reference Back

That was a pretty one, I heard you call
From the unsatisfactory hall
To the unsatisfactory room where I
Played record after record, idly,
Wasting my time at home, that you
Looked so much forward to.

Oliver's *Riverside Blues*, it was. And now
I shall, I suppose, always remember how
The flock of notes those antique Negroes blew
Out of Chicago air into
A huge remembering pre-electric horn
The year after I was born
Three decades later made this sudden bridge
From your unsatisfactory age
To my unsatisfactory prime.

Truly, though our element is time,
We are not suited to the long perspectives
Open at each instant of our lives.
They link us to our losses: worse,
They show us what we have as it once was,
Blindingly undiminished, just as though
By acting differently we could have kept it so.

Wild Oats

About twenty years ago
Two girls came in where I worked –
A bosomy English rose
And her friend in specs I could talk to.
Faces in those days sparked
The whole shooting-match off, and I doubt
If ever one had like hers:
But it was the friend I took out,

And in seven years after that
Wrote over four hundred letters,
Gave a ten-guinea ring
I got back in the end, and met
At numerous cathedral cities
Unknown to the clergy. I believe
I met beautiful twice. She was trying
Both times (so I thought) not to laugh.

Parting, after about five
Rehearsals, was an agreement
That I was too selfish, withdrawn,
And easily bored to love.
Well, useful to get that learnt.
In my wallet are still two snaps
Of bosomy rose with fur gloves on.
Unlucky charms, perhaps.

Essential Beauty

In frames as large as rooms that face all ways
And block the ends of streets with giant loaves,
Screen graves with custard, cover slums with praise
Of motor-oil and cuts of salmon, shine
Perpetually these sharply-pictured groves
Of how life should be. High above the gutter
A silver knife sinks into golden butter,
A glass of milk stands in a meadow, and
Well-balanced families, in fine
Midsummer weather, owe their smiles, their cars,
Even their youth, to that small cube each hand
Stretches towards. These, and the deep armchairs
Aligned to cups at bedtime, radiant bars
(Gas or electric), quarter-profile cats
By slippers on warm mats,
Reflect none of the rained-on streets and squares

They dominate outdoors. Rather, they rise
Serenely to proclaim pure crust, pure foam,
Pure coldness to our live imperfect eyes
That stare beyond this world, where nothing's made
As new or washed quite clean, seeking the home
All such inhabit. There, dark raftered pubs
Are filled with white-clothed ones from tennis-clubs,
And the boy puking his heart out in the Gents
Just missed them, as the pensioner paid
A halfpenny more for Granny Graveclothes' Tea
To taste old age, and dying smokers sense
Walking towards them through some dappled park
As if on water that unfocused she
No match lit up, nor drag ever brought near,
Who now stands newly clear,
Smiling, and recognising, and going dark.

Send No Money

Standing under the fobbed
Impendent belly of Time
Tell me the truth, I said,
Teach me the way things go.
All the other lads there
Were itching to have a bash
But I thought wanting unfair:
It and finding out clash.

So he patted my head, booming *Boy,*
There's no green in your eye:
Sit here, and watch the hail
Of occurrence clobber life out
To a shape no one sees –
Dare you look at that straight?
Oh thank you, I said, *Oh yes please,*
And sat down to wait.

Half life is over now,
And I meet full face on dark mornings
The bestial visor, bent in
By the blows of what happened to happen.
What does it prove? Sod all.
In this way I spent youth,
Tracing the trite untransferable
Truss-advertisement, truth.

Afternoons

Summer is fading:
The leaves fall in ones and twos
From trees bordering
The new recreation ground.
In the hollows of afternoons
Young mothers assemble
At swing and sandpit
Setting free their children.

Behind them, at intervals,
Stand husbands in skilled trades,
An estateful of washing,
And the albums, lettered
Our Wedding, lying
Near the television:
Before them, the wind
Is ruining their courting-places

That are still courting-places
(But the lovers are all in school),
And their children, so intent on
Finding more unripe acorns,
Expect to be taken home.
Their beauty has thickened.
Something is pushing them
To the side of their own lives.

An Arundel Tomb

Side by side, their faces blurred,
The earl and countess lie in stone,
Their proper habits vaguely shown
As jointed armour, stiffened pleat,
And that faint hint of the absurd –
The little dogs under their feet.

Such plainness of the pre-baroque
Hardly involves the eye, until
It meets his left-hand gauntlet, still
Clasped empty in the other; and
One sees, with a sharp tender shock,
His hand withdrawn, holding her hand.

They would not think to lie so long.
Such faithfulness in effigy
Was just a detail friends would see:
A sculptor's sweet commissioned grace
Thrown off in helping to prolong
The Latin names around the base.

They would not guess how early in
Their supine stationary voyage
The air would change to soundless damage,
Turn the old tenantry away;
How soon succeeding eyes begin
To look, not read. Rigidly they

Persisted, linked, through lengths and breadths
Of time. Snow fell, undated. Light
Each summer thronged the glass. A bright
Litter of birdcalls strewed the same
Bone-riddled ground. And up the paths
The endless altered people came,

Washing at their identity.
Now, helpless in the hollow of
An unarmorial age, a trough
Of smoke in slow suspended skeins
Above their scrap of history,
Only an attitude remains:

Time has transfigured them into
Untruth. The stone fidelity
They hardly meant has come to be
Their final blazon, and to prove
Our almost-instinct almost true:
What will survive of us is love.

HIGH WINDOWS

June 1974

To the Sea

To step over the low wall that divides
Road from concrete walk above the shore
Brings sharply back something known long before –
The miniature gaiety of seasides.
Everything crowds under the low horizon:
Steep beach, blue water, towels, red bathing caps,
The small hushed waves' repeated fresh collapse
Up the warm yellow sand, and further off
A white steamer stuck in the afternoon –

Still going on, all of it, still going on!
To lie, eat, sleep in hearing of the surf
(Ears to transistors, that sound tame enough
Under the sky), or gently up and down
Lead the uncertain children, frilled in white
And grasping at enormous air, or wheel
The rigid old along for them to feel
A final summer, plainly still occurs
As half an annual pleasure, half a rite,

As when, happy at being on my own,
I searched the sand for Famous Cricketers,
Or, farther back, my parents, listeners
To the same seaside quack, first became known.
Strange to it now, I watch the cloudless scene:
The same clear water over smoothed pebbles,
The distant bathers' weak protesting trebles
Down at its edge, and then the cheap cigars,
The chocolate-papers, tea-leaves, and, between

The rocks, the rusting soup-tins, till the first
Few families start the trek back to the cars.
The white steamer has gone. Like breathed-on glass
The sunlight has turned milky. If the worst

Of flawless weather is our falling short,
It may be that through habit these do best,
Coming to water clumsily undressed
Yearly; teaching their children by a sort
Of clowning; helping the old, too, as they ought.

Sympathy in White Major

When I drop four cubes of ice
Chimingly in a glass, and add
Three goes of gin, a lemon slice,
And let a ten-ounce tonic void
In foaming gulps until it smothers
Everything else up to the edge,
I lift the lot in private pledge:
He devoted his life to others.

While other people wore like clothes
The human beings in their days
I set myself to bring to those
Who thought I could the lost displays;
It didn't work for them or me,
But all concerned were nearer thus
(Or so we thought) to all the fuss
Than if we'd missed it separately.

A decent chap, a real good sort,
Straight as a die, one of the best,
A brick, a trump, a proper sport,
Head and shoulders above the rest;
How many lives would have been duller
Had he not been here below?
Here's to the whitest man I know –
Though white is not my favourite colour.

The Trees

The trees are coming into leaf
Like something almost being said;
The recent buds relax and spread,
Their greenness is a kind of grief.

Is it that they are born again
And we grow old? No, they die too.
Their yearly trick of looking new
Is written down in rings of grain.

Yet still the unresting castles thresh
In fullgrown thickness every May.
Last year is dead, they seem to say,
Begin afresh, afresh, afresh.

Livings

I deal with farmers, things like dips and feed.
Every third month I book myself in at
The —— Hotel in —ton for three days.
The boots carries my lean old leather case
Up to a single, where I hang my hat.
One beer, and then 'the dinner', at which I read
The —*shire Times* from soup to stewed pears.
Births, deaths. For sale. Police court. Motor spares.

Afterwards, whisky in the Smoke Room: Clough,
Margetts, the Captain, Dr. Watterson;
Who makes ends meet, who's taking the knock,
Government tariffs, wages, price of stock.
Smoke hangs under the light. The pictures on
The walls are comic – hunting, the trenches, stuff
Nobody minds or notices. A sound
Of dominoes from the Bar. I stand a round.

Later, the square is empty: a big sky
Drains down the estuary like the bed
Of a gold river, and the Customs House
Still has its office lit. I drowse
Between ex-Army sheets, wondering why
I think it's worthwhile coming. Father's dead:
He used to, but the business now is mine.
It's time for change, in nineteen twenty-nine.

II

Seventy feet down
The sea explodes upwards,
Relapsing, to slaver

Off landing-stage steps –
Running suds, rejoice!

Rocks writhe back to sight.
Mussels, limpets,
Husband their tenacity
In the freezing slither –
Creatures, I cherish you!

By day, sky builds
Grape-dark over the salt
Unsown stirring fields.
Radio rubs its legs,
Telling me of elsewhere:

Barometers falling,
Ports wind-shuttered,
Fleets pent like hounds,
Fires in humped inns
Kippering sea-pictures –

Keep it all off!
By night, snow swerves
(O loose moth world)
Through the stare travelling
Leather-black waters.

Guarded by brilliance
I set plate and spoon,
And after, divining-cards.
Lit shelved liners
Grope like mad worlds westward.

Tonight we dine without the Master
(Nocturnal vapours do not please);
The port goes round so much the faster,
Topics are raised with no less ease –
Which advowson looks the fairest,
What the wood from Snape will fetch,
Names for *pudendum mulieris*,
Why is Judas like Jack Ketch?

The candleflames grow thin, then broaden:
Our butler Starveling piles the logs
And sets behind the screen a jordan
(Quicker than going to the bogs).
The wine heats temper and complexion:
Oath-enforced assertions fly
On rheumy fevers, resurrection,
Regicide and rabbit pie.

The fields around are cold and muddy,
The cobbled streets close by are still,
A sizar shivers at his study,
The kitchen cat has made a kill;
The bells discuss the hour's gradations,
Dusty shelves hold prayers and proofs:
Above, Chaldean constellations
Sparkle over crowded roofs.

Forget What Did

Stopping the diary
Was a stun to memory,
Was a blank starting,

One no longer cicatrised
By such words, such actions
As bleakened waking.

I wanted them over,
Hurried to burial
And looked back on

Like the wars and winters
Missing behind the windows
Of an opaque childhood.

And the empty pages?
Should they ever be filled
Let it be with observed

Celestial recurrences,
The day the flowers come,
And when the birds go.

High Windows

When I see a couple of kids
And guess he's fucking her and she's
Taking pills or wearing a diaphragm,
I know this is paradise

Everyone old has dreamed of all their lives –
Bonds and gestures pushed to one side
Like an outdated combine harvester,
And everyone young going down the long slide

To happiness, endlessly. I wonder if
Anyone looked at me, forty years back,
And thought, *That'll be the life;*
No God any more, or sweating in the dark

About hell and that, or having to hide
What you think of the priest. He
And his lot will all go down the long slide
Like free bloody birds. And immediately

Rather than words comes the thought of high windows:
The sun-comprehending glass,
And beyond it, the deep blue air, that shows
Nothing, and is nowhere, and is endless.

Friday Night in the Royal Station Hotel

Light spreads darkly downwards from the high
Clusters of lights over empty chairs
That face each other, coloured differently.
Through open doors, the dining-room declares
A larger loneliness of knives and glass
And silence laid like carpet. A porter reads
An unsold evening paper. Hours pass,
And all the salesmen have gone back to Leeds,
Leaving full ashtrays in the Conference Room.

In shoeless corridors, the lights burn. How
Isolated, like a fort, it is –
The headed paper, made for writing home
(If home existed) letters of exile: *Now
Night comes on. Waves fold behind villages.*

The Old Fools

What do they think has happened, the old fools,
To make them like this? Do they somehow suppose
It's more grown-up when your mouth hangs open and drools,
And you keep on pissing yourself, and can't remember
Who called this morning? Or that, if they only chose,
They could alter things back to when they danced all night,
Or went to their wedding, or sloped arms some September?
Or do they fancy there's really been no change,
And they've always behaved as if they were crippled or tight,
Or sat through days of thin continuous dreaming
Watching light move? If they don't (and they can't), it's strange:
      Why aren't they screaming?

At death, you break up: the bits that were you
Start speeding away from each other for ever
With no one to see. It's only oblivion, true:
We had it before, but then it was going to end,
And was all the time merging with a unique endeavour
To bring to bloom the million-petalled flower
Of being here. Next time you can't pretend
There'll be anything else. And these are the first signs:
Not knowing how, not hearing who, the power
Of choosing gone. Their looks show that they're for it:
Ash hair, toad hands, prune face dried into lines –
      How can they ignore it?

Perhaps being old is having lighted rooms
Inside your head, and people in them, acting.
People you know, yet can't quite name; each looms
Like a deep loss restored, from known doors turning,
Setting down a lamp, smiling from a stair, extracting
A known book from the shelves; or sometimes only
The rooms themselves, chairs and a fire burning,
The blown bush at the window, or the sun's

Faint friendliness on the wall some lonely
Rain-ceased midsummer evening. That is where they live:
Not here and now, but where all happened once.
        This is why they give

An air of baffled absence, trying to be there
Yet being here. For the rooms grow farther, leaving
Incompetent cold, the constant wear and tear
Of taken breath, and them crouching below
Extinction's alp, the old fools, never perceiving
How near it is. This must be what keeps them quiet:
The peak that stays in view wherever we go
For them is rising ground. Can they never tell
What is dragging them back, and how it will end? Not at night?
Not when the strangers come? Never, throughout
The whole hideous inverted childhood? Well,
        We shall find out.

Going, Going

I thought it would last my time –
The sense that, beyond the town,
There would always be fields and farms,
Where the village louts could climb
Such trees as were not cut down;
I knew there'd be false alarms

In the papers about old streets
And split-level shopping, but some
Have always been left so far;
And when the old part retreats
As the bleak high-risers come
We can always escape in the car.

Things are tougher than we are, just
As earth will always respond
However we mess it about;
Chuck filth in the sea, if you must:
The tides will be clean beyond.
– But what do I feel now? Doubt?

Or age, simply? The crowd
Is young in the M1 café;
Their kids are screaming for more –
More houses, more parking allowed,
More caravan sites, more pay.
On the Business Page, a score

Of spectacled grins approve
Some takeover bid that entails
Five per cent profit (and ten
Per cent more in the estuaries): move
Your works to the unspoilt dales
(Grey area grants)! And when

You try to get near the sea
In summer...
                    It seems, just now,
To be happening so very fast;
Despite all the land left free
For the first time I feel somehow
That it isn't going to last,

That before I snuff it, the whole
Boiling will be bricked in
Except for the tourist parts –
First slum of Europe: a role
It won't be so hard to win,
With a cast of crooks and tarts.

And that will be England gone,
The shadows, the meadows, the lanes
The guildhalls, the carved choirs.
There'll be books; it will linger on
In galleries; but all that remains
For us will be concrete and tyres.

Most things are never meant.
This won't be, most likely: but greeds
And garbage are too thick-strewn
To be swept up now, or invent
Excuses that make them all needs.
I just think it will happen, soon.

The Card-Players

Jan van Hogspeuw staggers to the door
And pisses at the dark. Outside, the rain
Courses in cart-ruts down the deep mud lane.
Inside, Dirk Dogstoerd pours himself some more,
And holds a cinder to his clay with tongs,
Belching out smoke. Old Prijck snores with the gale,
His skull face firelit; someone behind drinks ale,
And opens mussels, and croaks scraps of songs
Towards the ham-hung rafters about love.
Dirk deals the cards. Wet century-wide trees
Clash in surrounding starlessness above
This lamplit cave, where Jan turns back and farts,
Gobs at the grate, and hits the queen of hearts.

Rain, wind and fire! The secret, bestial peace!

The Building

Higher than the handsomest hotel
The lucent comb shows up for miles, but see,
All round it close-ribbed streets rise and fall
Like a great sigh out of the last century.
The porters are scruffy; what keep drawing up
At the entrance are not taxis; and in the hall
As well as creepers hangs a frightening smell.

There are paperbacks, and tea at so much a cup,
Like an airport lounge, but those who tamely sit
On rows of steel chairs turning the ripped mags
Haven't come far. More like a local bus,
These outdoor clothes and half-filled shopping bags
And faces restless and resigned, although
Every few minutes comes a kind of nurse

To fetch someone away: the rest refit
Cups back to saucers, cough, or glance below
Seats for dropped gloves or cards. Humans, caught
On ground curiously neutral, homes and names
Suddenly in abeyance; some are young,
Some old, but most at that vague age that claims
The end of choice, the last of hope; and all

Here to confess that something has gone wrong.
It must be error of a serious sort,
For see how many floors it needs, how tall
It's grown by now, and how much money goes
In trying to correct it. See the time,
Half-past eleven on a working day,
And these picked out of it; see, as they climb

To their appointed levels, how their eyes
Go to each other, guessing; on the way

Someone's wheeled past, in washed-to-rags ward clothes:
They see him, too. They're quiet. To realise
This new thing held in common makes them quiet,
For past these doors are rooms, and rooms past those,
And more rooms yet, each one further off

And harder to return from; and who knows
Which he will see, and when? For the moment, wait,
Look down at the yard. Outside seems old enough:
Red brick, lagged pipes, and someone walking by it
Out to the car park, free. Then, past the gate,
Traffic; a locked church; short terraced streets
Where kids chalk games, and girls with hair-dos fetch

Their separates from the cleaners – O world,
Your loves, your chances, are beyond the stretch
Of any hand from here! And so, unreal,
A touching dream to which we all are lulled
But wake from separately. In it, conceits
And self-protecting ignorance congeal
To carry life, collapsing only when

Called to these corridors (for now once more
The nurse beckons –). Each gets up and goes
At last. Some will be out by lunch, or four;
Others, not knowing it, have come to join
The unseen congregations whose white rows
Lie set apart above – women, men;
Old, young; crude facets of the only coin

This place accepts. All know they are going to die.
Not yet, perhaps not here, but in the end,
And somewhere like this. That is what it means,
This clean-sliced cliff; a struggle to transcend
The thought of dying, for unless its powers

Outbuild cathedrals nothing contravenes
The coming dark, though crowds each evening try

With wasteful, weak, propitiatory flowers.

·

Posterity

Jake Balokowsky, my biographer,
Has this page microfilmed. Sitting inside
His air-conditioned cell at Kennedy
In jeans and sneakers, he's no call to hide
Some slight impatience with his destiny:
'I'm stuck with this old fart at least a year;

I wanted to teach school in Tel Aviv,
But Myra's folks' – he makes the money sign –
'Insisted I got tenure. When there's kids –'
He shrugs. 'It's stinking dead, the research line;
Just let me put this bastard on the skids,
I'll get a couple of semesters leave

To work on Protest Theater.' They both rise,
Make for the Coke dispenser. 'What's he like?
Christ, I just told you. Oh, you know the thing,
That crummy textbook stuff from Freshman Psych,
Not out of kicks or something happening –
One of those old-type *natural* fouled-up guys.'

Dublinesque

Down stucco sidestreets,
Where light is pewter
And afternoon mist
Brings lights on in shops
Above race-guides and rosaries,
A funeral passes.

The hearse is ahead,
But after there follows
A troop of streetwalkers
In wide flowered hats,
Leg-of-mutton sleeves,
And ankle-length dresses.

There is an air of great friendliness,
As if they were honouring
One they were fond of;
Some caper a few steps,
Skirts held skilfully
(Someone claps time),

And of great sadness also.
As they wend away
A voice is heard singing
Of Kitty, or Katy,
As if the name meant once
All love, all beauty.

Homage to a Government

Next year we are to bring the soldiers home
For lack of money, and it is all right.
Places they guarded, or kept orderly,
Must guard themselves, and keep themselves orderly.
We want the money for ourselves at home
Instead of working. And this is all right.

It's hard to say who wanted it to happen,
But now it's been decided nobody minds.
The places are a long way off, not here,
Which is all right, and from what we hear
The soldiers there only made trouble happen.
Next year we shall be easier in our minds.

Next year we shall be living in a country
That brought its soldiers home for lack of money.
The statues will be standing in the same
Tree-muffled squares, and look nearly the same.
Our children will not know it's a different country.
All we can hope to leave them now is money.

1969

This Be The Verse

They fuck you up, your mum and dad.
　They may not mean to, but they do.
They fill you with the faults they had
　And add some extra, just for you.

But they were fucked up in their turn
　By fools in old-style hats and coats,
Who half the time were soppy-stern
　And half at one another's throats.

Man hands on misery to man.
　It deepens like a coastal shelf.
Get out as early as you can,
　And don't have any kids yourself.

How Distant

How distant, the departure of young men
Down valleys, or watching
The green shore past the salt-white cordage
Rising and falling,

Cattlemen, or carpenters, or keen
Simply to get away
From married villages before morning,
Melodeons play

On tiny decks past fraying cliffs of water
Or late at night
Sweet under the differently-swung stars,
When the chance sight

Of a girl doing her laundry in the steerage
Ramifies endlessly.
This is being young,
Assumption of the startled century

Like new store clothes,
The huge decisions printed out by feet
Inventing where they tread,
The random windows conjuring a street.

Sad Steps

Groping back to bed after a piss
I part thick curtains, and am startled by
The rapid clouds, the moon's cleanliness.

Four o'clock: wedge-shadowed gardens lie
Under a cavernous, a wind-picked sky.
There's something laughable about this,

The way the moon dashes through clouds that blow
Loosely as cannon-smoke to stand apart
(Stone-coloured light sharpening the roofs below)

High and preposterous and separate –
Lozenge of love! Medallion of art!
O wolves of memory! Immensements! No,

One shivers slightly, looking up there.
The hardness and the brightness and the plain
Far-reaching singleness of that wide stare

Is a reminder of the strength and pain
Of being young; that it can't come again,
But is for others undiminished somewhere.

Solar

Suspended lion face
Spilling at the centre
Of an unfurnished sky
How still you stand,
And how unaided
Single stalkless flower
You pour unrecompensed.

The eye sees you
Simplified by distance
Into an origin,
Your petalled head of flames
Continuously exploding.
Heat is the echo of your
Gold.

Coined there among
Lonely horizontals
You exist openly.
Our needs hourly
Climb and return like angels.
Unclosing like a hand,
You give for ever.

Annus Mirabilis

Sexual intercourse began
In nineteen sixty-three
(Which was rather late for me) –
Between the end of the *Chatterley* ban
And the Beatles' first LP.

Up till then there'd only been
A sort of bargaining,
A wrangle for a ring,
A shame that started at sixteen
And spread to everything.

Then all at once the quarrel sank:
Everyone felt the same,
And every life became
A brilliant breaking of the bank,
A quite unlosable game.

So life was never better than
In nineteen sixty-three
(Though just too late for me) –
Between the end of the *Chatterley* ban
And the Beatles' first LP.

Vers de Société

My wife and I have asked a crowd of craps
To come and waste their time and ours: perhaps
You'd care to join us? In a pig's arse, friend.
Day comes to an end.
The gas fire breathes, the trees are darkly swayed.
And so *Dear Warlock-Williams: I'm afraid –*

Funny how hard it is to be alone.
I could spend half my evenings, if I wanted,
Holding a glass of washing sherry, canted
Over to catch the drivel of some bitch
Who's read nothing but *Which*;
Just think of all the spare time that has flown

Straight into nothingness by being filled
With forks and faces, rather than repaid
Under a lamp, hearing the noise of wind,
And looking out to see the moon thinned
To an air-sharpened blade.
A life, and yet how sternly it's instilled

All solitude is selfish. No one now
Believes the hermit with his gown and dish
Talking to God (who's gone too); the big wish
Is to have people nice to you, which means
Doing it back somehow.
Virtue is social. Are, then, these routines

Playing at goodness, like going to church?
Something that bores us, something we don't do well
(Asking that ass about his fool research)
But try to feel, because, however crudely,
It shows us what should be?
Too subtle, that. Too decent, too. Oh hell,

Only the young can be alone freely.
The time is shorter now for company,
And sitting by a lamp more often brings
Not peace, but other things.
Beyond the light stand failure and remorse
Whispering *Dear Warlock-Williams: Why, of course –*

Show Saturday

Grey day for the Show, but cars jam the narrow lanes.
Inside, on the field, judging has started: dogs
(Set their legs back, hold out their tails) and ponies (manes
Repeatedly smoothed, to calm heads); over there, sheep
(Cheviot and Blackface); by the hedge, squealing logs
(Chain Saw Competition). Each has its own keen crowd.
In the main arena, more judges meet by a jeep:
The jumping's on next. Announcements, splutteringly loud,

Clash with the quack of a man with pound notes round his hat
And a lit-up board. There's more than just animals:
Bead-stalls, balloon-men, a Bank; a beer-marquee that
Half-screens a canvas Gents; a tent selling tweed,
And another, jackets. Folks sit about on bales
Like great straw dice. For each scene is linked by spaces
Not given to anything much, where kids scrap, freed,
While their owners stare different ways with incurious faces.

The wrestling starts, late; a wide ring of people; then cars;
Then trees; then pale sky. Two young men in acrobats' tights
And embroidered trunks hug each other; rock over the grass,
Stiff-legged, in a two-man scrum. One falls: they shake hands.
Two more start, one grey-haired: he wins, though. They're not
    so much fights
As long immobile strainings that end in unbalance
With one on his back, unharmed, while the other stands
Smoothing his hair. But there are other talents –

The long high tent of growing and making, wired-off
Wood tables past which crowds shuffle, eyeing the scrubbed
    spaced
Extrusions of earth: blanch leeks like church candles, six pods of
Broad beans (one split open), dark shining-leafed cabbages – rows
Of single supreme versions, followed (on laced

Paper mats) by dairy and kitchen; four brown eggs, four white
   eggs,
Four plain scones, four dropped scones, pure excellences that
   enclose
A recession of skills. And, after them, lambing-sticks, rugs,

Needlework, knitted caps, baskets, all worthy, all well done,
But less than the honeycombs. Outside, the jumping's over.
The young ones thunder their ponies in competition
Twice round the ring; then trick races, Musical Stalls,
Sliding off, riding bareback, the ponies dragged to and fro for
Bewildering requirements, not minding. But now, in the
   background,
Like shifting scenery, horse-boxes move; each crawls
Towards the stock entrance, tilting and swaying, bound

For far-off farms. The pound-note man decamps.
The car park has thinned. They're loading jumps on a truck.
Back now to private addresses, gates and lamps
In high stone one-street villages, empty at dusk,
And side roads of small towns (sports finals stuck
In front doors, allotments reaching down to the railway);
Back now to autumn, leaving the ended husk
Of summer that brought them here for Show Saturday –

The men with hunters, dog-breeding wool-defined women,
Children all saddle-swank, mugfaced middleaged wives
Glaring at jellies, husbands on leave from the garden
Watchful as weasels, car-tuning curt-haired sons –
Back now, all of them, to their local lives:
To names on vans, and business calendars
Hung up in kitchens; back to loud occasions
In the Corn Exchange, to market days in bars,

To winter coming, as the dismantled Show
Itself dies back into the area of work.

Let it stay hidden there like strength, below
Sale-bills and swindling; something people do,
Not noticing how time's rolling smithy-smoke
Shadows much greater gestures; something they share
That breaks ancestrally each year into
Regenerate union. Let it always be there.

Money

Quarterly, is it, money reproaches me:
  'Why do you let me lie here wastefully?
I am all you never had of goods and sex.
  You could get them still by writing a few cheques.'

So I look at others, what they do with theirs:
  They certainly don't keep it upstairs.
By now they've a second house and car and wife:
  Clearly money has something to do with life

— In fact, they've a lot in common, if you enquire:
  You can't put off being young until you retire,
And however you bank your screw, the money you save
  Won't in the end buy you more than a shave.

I listen to money singing. It's like looking down
  From long french windows at a provincial town,
The slums, the canal, the churches ornate and mad
  In the evening sun. It is intensely sad.

Cut Grass

Cut grass lies frail:
Brief is the breath
Mown stalks exhale.
Long, long the death

It dies in the white hours
Of young-leafed June
With chestnut flowers,
With hedges snowlike strewn,

White lilac bowed,
Lost lanes of Queen Anne's lace,
And that high-builded cloud
Moving at summer's pace.

The Explosion

On the day of the explosion
Shadows pointed towards the pithead:
In the sun the slagheap slept.

Down the lane came men in pitboots
Coughing oath-edged talk and pipe-smoke,
Shouldering off the freshened silence.

One chased after rabbits; lost them;
Came back with a nest of lark's eggs;
Showed them; lodged them in the grasses.

So they passed in beards and moleskins,
Fathers, brothers, nicknames, laughter,
Through the tall gates standing open.

At noon, there came a tremor; cows
Stopped chewing for a second; sun,
Scarfed as in a heat-haze, dimmed.

The dead go on before us, they
Are sitting in God's house in comfort,
We shall see them face to face –

Plain as lettering in the chapels
It was said, and for a second
Wives saw men of the explosion

Larger than in life they managed –
Gold as on a coin, or walking
Somehow from the sun towards them,

One showing the eggs unbroken.

APPENDIX I

Uncollected Poems
1940–1972

Ultimatum

But we must build our walls, for what we are
Necessitates it, and we must construct
The ship to navigate behind them, there.
Hopeless to ignore, helpless instruct
For any term of time beyond the years
That warn us of the need for emigration:
Exploded the ancient saying: Life is yours.

For on our island is no railway station,
There are no tickets for the Vale of Peace,
No docks where trading ships and seagulls pass.

Remember stories you read when a boy
– The shipwrecked sailor gaining safety by
His knife, treetrunk, and lianas – for now
You must escape, or perish saying no.

Story

Tired of a landscape known too well when young:
The deliberate shallow hills, the boring birds
Flying past rocks; tired of remembering
The village children and their naughty words,
He abandoned his small holding and went South,
Recognised at once his wished-for lie
In the inhabitants' attractive mouth,
The church beside the marsh, the hot blue sky.

Settled. And in this mirage lived his dreams,
The friendly bully, saint, or lovely chum
According to his moods. Yet he at times
Would think about his village, and would wonder
If the children and the rocks were still the same.

But he forgot all this as he grew older.

A Writer

'Interesting, but futile,' said his diary,
Where day by day his movements were recorded
And nothing but his loves received inquiry;
He knew, of course, no actions were rewarded,
There were no prizes: though the eye could see
Wide beauty in a motion or a pause,
It need expect no lasting salary
Beyond the bowels' momentary applause.

He lived for years and never was surprised:
A member of his foolish, lying race
Explained away their vices: realised
It was a gift that he possessed alone:
To look the world directly in the face;
The face he did not see to be his own.

May Weather

A month ago in fields
Rehearsals were begun;
The stage that summer builds
And confidently holds
Was floodlit by the sun
And habited by men.

But parts were not correct:
The gestures of the crowd
Invented to attract
Need practice to perfect,
And balancing of cloud
With sunlight must be made;

So awkward was this May
Then training to prepare
Summer's impressive lie –
Upon whose every day
So many ruined are
May could not make aware.

Observation

Only in books the flat and final happens,
Only in dreams we meet and interlock,
The hand impervious to nervous shock,
The future proofed against our vain suspense;

But since the tideline of the incoming past
Is where we walk, and it is air we breathe,
Remember then our only shape is death
When mask and face are nailed apart at last.

Range-finding laughter, and ambush of tears,
Machine-gun practice on the heart's desires
Speak of a government of medalled fears.

Shake, wind, the branches of their crooked wood,
Where much is picturesque but nothing good,
And nothing can be found for poor men's fires.

Disintegration

Time running beneath the pillow wakes
Lovers entrained who in the name of love
Were promised the steeples and fanlights of a dream;
Joins the renters of each single room
Across the tables to observe a life
Dissolving in the acid of their sex;

Time that scatters hair upon a head
Spreads the ice sheet on the shaven lawn;
Signing an annual permit for the frost
Ploughs the stubble in the land at last
To introduce the unknown to the known
And only by politeness make them breed;

Time over the roofs of what has nearly been
Circling, a migratory, static bird,
Predicts no change in future's lancing shape,
And daylight shows the streets still tangled up;
Time points the simian camera in the head
Upon confusion to be seen and seen.

Mythological Introduction

A white girl lay on the grass
With her arms held out for love;
Her goldbrown hair fell down her face,
And her two lips move:

See, I am the whitest cloud that strays
Through a deep sky:
I am your senses' crossroads,
Where the four seasons lie.

She rose up in the middle of the lawn
And spread her arms wide;
And the webbed earth where she had lain
Had eaten away her side.

A Stone Church Damaged by a Bomb

Planted deeper than roots,
This chiselled, flung-up faith
Runs and leaps against the sky,
A prayer killed into stone
Among the always-dying trees;
Windows throw back the sun
And hands are folded in their work at peace,
Though where they lie
The dead are shapeless in the shapeless earth.

Because, though taller the elms,
It forever rejects the soil,
Because its suspended bells
Beat when the birds are dumb,
And men are buried, and leaves burnt
Every indifferent autumn,
I have looked on that proud front
And the calm locked into walls,
I have worshipped that whispering shell.

Yet the wound, O see the wound
This petrified heart has taken,
Because, created deathless,
Nothing but death remained
To scatter magnificence;
And now what scaffolded mind
Can rebuild experience
As coral is set budding under seas,
Though none, O none sees what patterns it is making?

Femmes Damnées

The fire is ash: the early morning sun
Outlines the patterns on the curtains, drawn
The night before. The milk's been on the step,
The *Guardian* in the letter-box, since dawn.

Upstairs, the beds have not been touched, and thence
Builders' estates and the main road are seen,
With labourers, petrol-pumps, a Green Line bus,
And plots of cabbages set in between.

But the living-room is ruby: there upon
Cushions from Harrods, strewn in tumbled heaps
Around the floor, smelling of smoke and wine,
Rosemary sits. Her hands are clasped. She weeps.

She stares about her: round the decent walls
(The ribbon lost, her pale gold hair falls down)
Sees books and photos: 'Dance'; 'The Rhythmic Life';
Miss Rachel Wilson in a cap and gown.

Stretched out before her, Rachel curls and curves,
Eyelids and lips apart, her glances filled
With satisfied ferocity; she smiles,
As beasts smile on the prey they have just killed.

The marble clock has stopped. The curtained sun
Burns on: the room grows hot. There, it appears,
A vase of flowers has spilt, and soaked away.
The only sound heard is the sound of tears.

Plymouth

A box of teak, a box of sandalwood,
A brass-ringed spyglass in a case,
A coin, leaf-thin with many polishings,
Last kingdom of a gold forgotten face,
These lie about the room, and daily shine
When new-built ships set out towards the sun.

If they had any roughness, any flaw,
An unfamiliar scent, all this has gone;
They are no more than ornaments, or eyes,
No longer knowing what they looked upon,
Turned sightless; rivers of Eden, rivers of blood
Once blinded them, and were not understood.

The hands that chose them rust upon a stick.
Let my hands find such symbols, that can be
Unnoticed in the casual light of day,
Lying in wait for half a century
To split chance lives across, that had not dreamed
Such coasts had echoed, or such seabirds screamed.

Portrait

Her hands intend no harm:
Her hands devote themselves
To sheltering a flame;
Winds are her enemies,
And everything that strives
To bring her cold and darkness.

But wax and wick grow short:
These she so dearly guards
Despite her care die out;
Her hands are not strong enough
Her hands will fall to her sides
And no wind will trouble to break her grief.

The Dedicated

Some must employ the scythe
Upon the grasses,
That the walks be smooth
For the feet of the angel.
Some keep in repair
The locks, that the visitor
Unhindered passes
To the innermost chamber.

Some have for endeavour
To sign away life
As lover to lover,
Or a bird using its wings
To fly to the fowler's compass,
Not out of willingness,
But being aware of
Eternal requirings.

And if they have leave
To pray, it is for contentment
If the feet of the dove
Perch on the scythe's handle,
Perch once, and then depart
Their knowledge. After, they wait
Only the colder advent,
The quenching of candles.

Modesties

Words as plain as hen-birds' wings
Do not lie,
Do not over-broider things –
Are too shy.

Thoughts that shuffle round like pence
Through each reign,
Wear down to their simplest sense,
Yet remain.

Weeds are not supposed to grow,
But by degrees
Some achieve a flower, although
No one sees.

Fiction and the Reading Public

Give me a thrill, says the reader,
Give me a kick;
I don't care how you succeed, or
What subject you pick.
Choose something you know all about
That'll sound like real life:
Your childhood, your Dad pegging out,
How you sleep with your wife.

But that's not sufficient, unless
You make me feel good –
Whatever you're 'trying to express'
Let it be understood
That 'somehow' God plaits up the threads,
Makes 'all for the best',
That we may lie quiet in our beds
And not be 'depressed'.

For I call the tune in this racket:
I pay your screw,
Write reviews and the bull on the jacket –
So stop looking blue
And start serving up your sensations
Before it's too late;
Just please me for two generations –
You'll be 'truly great'.

Oils

Sun. Tree. Beginning. God in a thicket. Crown.
Never-abdicated constellation. Blood.
Barn-clutch of life. Trigger of the future.
Magic weed the doctor shakes in the dance.
Many rains and many rivers, making one river.
Password. Installation. Root of tongues.

Working-place to which the small seed is guided,
Inlet unvisited by marine biologist,
Entire alternative in man and woman
Opening at a touch like a water-flower,
New voice saying new words at a new speed
From which the future erupts like struck oil,

No one can migrate across your boundaries.
No one can exist without a habit for you.
No one can tear your thread out of himself.
No one can tie you down or set you free.
Apart from your tribe, there is only the dead,
And even them you grip and begin to use.

'Who called love conquering'

Who called love conquering,
When its sweet flower
So easily dries among the sour
Lanes of the living?

Flowerless demonstrative weeds
Selfishly spread,
The white bride drowns in her bed
And tiny curled greeds

Grapple the sun down
By three o'clock
When the dire cloak of dark
Stiffens the town.

'Since the majority of me'

Since the majority of me
Rejects the majority of you,
Debating ends forthwith, and we
Divide. And sure of what to do

We disinfect new blocks of days
For our majorities to rent
With unshared friends and unwalked ways.
But silence too is eloquent:

A silence of minorities
That, unopposed at last, return
Each night with cancelled promises
They want renewed. They never learn.

Arrival

Morning, a glass door, flashes
Gold names off the new city,
Whose white shelves and domes travel
The slow sky all day.
I land to stay here;
And the windows flock open
And the curtains fly out like doves
And the past dries in a wind.

Now let me lie down, under
A wide-branched indifference,
Shovel faces like pennies
Down the back of mind,
Find voices coined to
An argot of motor-horns,
And let the cluttered-up houses
Keep their thick lives to themselves.

For this ignorance of me
Seems a kind of innocence.
Fast enough I shall wound it:
Let me breathe till then
Its milk-aired Eden,
Till my own life impound it –
Slow-falling; grey-veil-hung; a theft,
A style of dying only.

Tops

Tops heel and yaw,
Sent newly spinning:
Squirm round the floor
At the beginning,
Then draw gravely up
Like candle-flames, till
They are soundless, asleep,
Moving, yet still.
So they run on,
Until, with a falter,
A flicker – soon gone –
Their pace starts to alter:
Heeling again
As if hopelessly tired
They wobble, and then
The poise we admired
Reels, clatters and sprawls,
Pathetically over.
– And what most appals
Is that tiny first shiver,
That stumble, whereby
We know beyond doubt
They have almost run out
And are starting to die.

Success Story

To fail (transitive and intransitive)
I find to mean *be missing, disappoint,*
Or *not succeed in the attainment of*
(As in this case, *f. to do what I want*);
They trace it from the Latin *to deceive* . . .

Yes. But it wasn't that I played unfair:
Under fourteen, I sent in six words
My Chief Ambition to the Editor
With the signed promise about afterwards –
I undertake rigidly to forswear

The diet of this world, all rich game
And fat forbidding fruit, go by the board
Until – But that *until* has never come,
And I am starving where I always did.
Time to fall to, I fancy: long past time.

The explanation goes like this, in daylight:
To be ambitious is to fall in love
With a particular life you haven't got
And (since love picks your opposite) won't achieve.
That's clear as day. But come back late at night,

You'll hear a curious counter-whispering:
Success, it says, you've scored a great success.
Your wish has flowered, you've dodged the dirty feeding,
Clean past it now at hardly any price –
Just some pretence about the other thing.

Continuing to Live

Continuing to live – that is, repeat
A habit formed to get necessaries –
Is nearly always losing, or going without.
  It varies.

This loss of interest, hair, and enterprise –
Ah, if the game were poker, yes,
You might discard them, draw a full house!
  But it's chess.

And once you have walked the length of your mind, what
You command is clear as a lading-list.
Anything else must not, for you, be thought
  To exist.

And what's the profit? Only that, in time,
We half-identify the blind impress
All our behavings bear, may trace it home.
  But to confess,

On that green evening when our death begins,
Just what it was, is hardly satisfying,
Since it applied only to one man once,
  And that one dying.

Pigeons

On shallow slates the pigeons shift together,
Backing against a thin rain from the west
Blown across each sunk head and settled feather.
Huddling round the warm stack suits them best,
Till winter daylight weakens, and they grow
Hardly defined against the brickwork. Soon,
Light from a small intense lopsided moon
Shows them, black as their shadows, sleeping so.

Breadfruit

Boys dream of native girls who bring breadfruit,
    Whatever they are,
As bribes to teach them how to execute
Sixteen sexual positions on the sand;
This makes them join (the boys) the tennis club,
Jive at the Mecca, use deodorants, and
On Saturdays squire ex-schoolgirls to the pub
    By private car.

Such uncorrected visions end in church
    Or registrar:
A mortgaged semi- with a silver birch;
Nippers; the widowed mum; having to scheme
With money; illness; age. So absolute
Maturity falls, when old men sit and dream
Of naked native girls who bring breadfuit,
    Whatever they are.

Love

The difficult part of love
Is being selfish enough,
Is having the blind persistence
To upset an existence
Just for your own sake.
What cheek it must take.

And then the unselfish side –
How can you be satisfied,
Putting someone else first
So that you come off worst?
My life is for me.
As well ignore gravity.

Still, vicious or virtuous,
Love suits most of us.
Only the bleeder found
Selfish this wrong way round
Is ever wholly rebuffed,
And he can get stuffed.

'When the Russian tanks roll westward'

When the Russian tanks roll westward, what defence for you
  and me?
Colonel Sloman's Essex Rifles? The Light Horse of L.S.E.?

How

How high they build hospitals!
Lighted cliffs, against dawns
Of days people will die on.
I can see one from here.

How cold winter keeps
And long, ignoring
Our need now for kindness.
Spring has got into the wrong year.

How few people are,
Held apart by acres
Of housing, and children
With their shallow violent eyes.

Heads in the Women's Ward

On pillow after pillow lies
The wild white hair and staring eyes;
Jaws stand open; necks are stretched
With every tendon sharply sketched;
A bearded mouth talks silently
To someone no one else can see.

Sixty years ago they smiled
At lover, husband, first-born child.

Smiles are for youth. For old age come
Death's terror and delirium.

APPENDIX II

Uncollected Poems
1974–1984

The Life with a Hole in it

When I throw back my head and howl
People (women mostly) say
But you've always done what you want,
You always get your own way
– A perfectly vile and foul
Inversion of all that's been.
What the old ratbags mean
Is I've never done what I don't.

So the shit in the shuttered château
Who does his five hundred words
Then parts out the rest of the day
Between bathing and booze and birds
Is far off as ever, but so
Is that spectacled schoolteaching sod
(Six kids, and the wife in pod,
And her parents coming to stay) . . .

Life is an immobile, locked,
Three-handed struggle between
Your wants, the world's for you, and (worse)
The unbeatable slow machine
That brings what you'll get. Blocked,
They strain round a hollow stasis
Of havings-to, fear, faces.
Days sift down it constantly. Years.

Bridge for the Living

The words of a cantata composed by Anthony Hedges to celebrate the opening of the Humber Bridge, first performed at the City Hall in Hull on 11 April 1981

Isolate city spread alongside water,
Posted with white towers, she keeps her face
Half-turned to Europe, lonely northern daughter,
Holding through centuries her separate place.

Behind her domes and cranes enormous skies
Of gold and shadows build; a filigree
Of wharves and wires, ricks and refineries,
Her working skyline wanders to the sea.

In her remote three-cornered hinterland
Long white-flowered lanes follow the riverside.
The hills bend slowly seaward, plain gulls stand,
Sharp fox and brilliant pheasant walk, and wide

Wind-muscled wheatfields wash round villages,
Their churches half-submerged in leaf. They lie
Drowned in high summer, cartways and cottages,
The soft huge haze of ash-blue sea close by.

Snow-thickened winter days are yet more still:
Farms fold in fields, their single lamps come on,
Tall church-towers parley, airily audible,
Howden and Beverley, Hedon and Patrington,

While scattered on steep seas, ice-crusted ships
Like errant birds carry her loneliness,
A lighted memory no miles eclipse,
A harbour for the heart against distress.

*

And now this stride into our solitude,
A swallow-fall and rise of one plain line,
A giant step for ever to include
All our dear landscape in a new design.

The winds play on it like a harp; the song,
Sharp from the east, sun-throated from the west,
Will never to one separate shire belong,
But north and south make union manifest.

Lost centuries of local lives that rose
And flowered to fall short where they began
Seem now to reassemble and unclose,
All resurrected in this single span,

Reaching for the world, as our lives do,
As all lives do, reaching that we may give
The best of what we are and hold as true:
Always it is by bridges that we live.

Aubade

I work all day, and get half-drunk at night.
Waking at four to soundless dark, I stare.
In time the curtain-edges will grow light.
Till then I see what's really always there:
Unresting death, a whole day nearer now,
Making all thought impossible but how
And where and when I shall myself die.
Arid interrogation: yet the dread
Of dying, and being dead,
Flashes afresh to hold and horrify.

The mind blanks at the glare. Not in remorse
– The good not done, the love not given, time
Torn off unused – nor wretchedly because
An only life can take so long to climb
Clear of its wrong beginnings, and may never;
But at the total emptiness for ever,
The sure extinction that we travel to
And shall be lost in always. Not to be here,
Not to be anywhere,
And soon; nothing more terrible, nothing more true.

This is a special way of being afraid
No trick dispels. Religion used to try,
That vast moth-eaten musical brocade
Created to pretend we never die,
And specious stuff that says *No rational being*
Can fear a thing it will not feel, not seeing
That this is what we fear – no sight, no sound,
No touch or taste or smell, nothing to think with,
Nothing to love or link with,
The anaesthetic from which none come round.

And so it stays just on the edge of vision,
A small unfocused blur, a standing chill
That slows each impulse down to indecision.
Most things may never happen: this one will,
And realisation of it rages out
In furnace-fear when we are caught without
People or drink. Courage is no good:
It means not scaring others. Being brave
Lets no one off the grave.
Death is no different whined at than withstood.

Slowly light strengthens, and the room takes shape.
It stands plain as a wardrobe, what we know,
Have always known, know that we can't escape,
Yet can't accept. One side will have to go.
Meawhile telephones crouch, getting ready to ring
In locked-up offices, and all the uncaring
Intricate rented world begins to rouse.
The sky is white as clay, with no sun.
Work has to be done.
Postmen like doctors go from house to house.

1952–1977

In times when nothing stood
but worsened, or grew strange,
there was one constant good:
    she did not change.

'New eyes each year'

New eyes each year
Find old books here,
And new books, too,
Old eyes renew;
So youth and age
Like ink and page
In this house join,
Minting new coin.

The Mower

The mower stalled, twice; kneeling, I found
A hedgehog jammed up against the blades,
Killed. It had been in the long grass.

I had seen it before, and even fed it, once.
Now I had mauled its unobtrusive world
Unmendably. Burial was no help:

Next morning I got up and it did not.
The first day after a death, the new absence
Is always the same; we should be careful

Of each other, we should be kind
While there is still time.

'Dear CHARLES, My Muse, asleep or dead'

Dear CHARLES, My Muse, asleep or dead,
Offers this doggerel instead
To carry from the frozen North
Warm greetings for the twenty-fourth
Of lucky August, best of months
For us, as for that Roman once –
For you're a Leo, same as me
(Isn't it comforting to be
So lordly, selfish, vital, strong?
Or do you think they've got it wrong?),
And may its golden hours portend
As many years for you to spend.

One of the sadder things, I think,
Is how our birthdays slowly sink:
Presents and parties disappear,
The cards grow fewer year by year,
Till, when one reaches sixty-five,
How many care we're still alive?
Ah, CHARLES, be reassured! For you
Make lasting friends with all you do,
And all you write; your truth and sense
We count on as a sure defence
Against the trendy and the mad,
The feeble and the downright bad.
I hope you have a splendid day,
Acclaimed by wheeling gulls at play
And barking seals, sea-lithe and lazy
(My view of Cornwall's rather hazy),
And humans who don't think it sinful
To mark your birthday with a skinful.

Although I'm trying very hard
To sound unlike a birthday card,

That's all this is: so you may find it
Full of all that lies behind it –
Admiration; friendship too;
And hope that in the future you
Reap ever richer revenue.

'By day, a lifted study-storehouse'

By day, a lifted study-storehouse; night
  Converts it to a flattened cube of light.
Whichever's shown, the symbol is the same:
  Knowledge; a University; a name.

Party Politics

I never remember holding a full drink.
   My first look shows the level half-way down.
What next? Ration the rest, and try to think
   Of higher things, until mine host comes round?

Some people say, best show an empty glass:
   Someone will fill it. Well, I've tried that too.
You may get drunk, or dry half-hours may pass.
   It seems to turn on where you are. Or who.

APPENDIX III

Composition Dates and Dates
of First Appearance

Dry-Point   17 March 1950
  (originally the second of 'Two Portraits of
  Sex', as 'Etching') *XX Poems*, 1951
Next, Please   10 January 1951
  XX Poems, 1951
Going   February? 1946
  XX Poems, 1951
Wants   1 June 1950
  XX Poems, 1951
Maiden Name   15 January 1955
Born Yesterday   20 January 1954
  Spectator, 30 July 1954
Whatever Happened?   26 October 1953
  BBC Third Programme, 'New Verse',
  8 April 1954 (as 'What Next'); *FP 21*, 1954
No Road   28 October 1950
  XX Poems, 1951
Wires   4 November 1950
  XX Poems, 1951
Church Going   28 July 1954
  Spectator, 18 November 1955
Age   26 May 1954
  Spectator, 2 July 1954
Myxomatosis   1954?
  Spectator, 26 November 1954
Toads   16 March 1954
  Listen, Summer 1954
Poetry of Departures   23 January 1954
  Poetry & Audience, 10 June 1954
Triple Time   3 October 1953
  Poetry & Audience, 28 January 1954
Spring   19 May 1950
  XX Poems, 1951
Deceptions   20 February 1950
  XX Poems, 1951

Home is so Sad   31 December 1958
   Listener, 23 January 1964
Toads Revisited   October 1962
   Spectator, 23 November 1962
Water   6 April 1954
   Listen, Summer–Autumn 1957
The Whitsun Weddings   18 October 1958
   'New Poetry' (BBC Third Programme),
   5 April 1959; *Encounter*, June 1959
Self's the Man   5 November 1958
Take One Home for the Kiddies   13 August 1960
   Listener, 5 December 1963
Days   3 August 1953
   Listen, Summer–Autumn 1957
MCMXIV   17 May 1960
   Saturday Book, 1960
Talking in Bed   10 August 1960
   Texas Quarterly, Winter 1960
The Large Cool Store   18 June 1961
   Times Literary Supplement, 14 July 1961
A Study of Reading Habits   20 August 1960
   Critical Quarterly, Winter 1960
As Bad as a Mile   9 February 1960
   Audit (University of Buffalo), 28 March
   1961 (as 'As Good as a Mile')
Ambulances   10 January 1961
   'New Poetry' (BBC Third Programme),
   March 1961; *London Magazine*, April 1961
The Importance of Elsewhere   13 June 1955
   BBC Third Programme ('Three Modern
   Poets'), 16 August 1955; *Listener*,
   8 September 1955
Sunny Prestatyn   October? 1962
   London Magazine, January 1963

First Sight	3 March 1956
Times Educational Supplement (as 'At First'), 13 July 1956	
Dockery and Son	28 March 1963
Listener, 11 April 1963	
Ignorance	11 September 1955
Listen, Summer 1956	
Reference Back	21 August 1955
Listen (as 'Referred Back'), Autumn 1955	
Wild Oats	12 May 1962
the Review, February 1963	
Essential Beauty	26 June 1962
Spectator, 5 October 1962	
Send No Money	21 August 1962
Observer, 18 November 1962	
Afternoons	September? 1959
Listen (as 'Before Tea'), Spring 1960	
An Arundel Tomb	20 February 1956
London Magazine, May 1956	

HIGH WINDOWS

To the Sea	October 1969
London Magazine, January 1970	
Sympathy in White Major	31 August 1967
London Magazine, December 1967	
The Trees	2 June 1967
New Statesman, 17 May 1968	
Livings I	16 October 1971
Observer, 20 February 1972	
Livings II	23 November 1971
Observer, 20 February 1972	
Livings III	10 December 1971
Observer, 20 February 1972	
Forget What Did	6 August 1971
High Windows	

High Windows 12 February 1967
Word in the Desert, 1968
Friday Night in the Royal Station Hotel 20 May 1966
Sheffield Morning Telegraph, 7 January 1967
The Old Fools 12 January 1973
The Listener, 1 February 1973
Going, Going 25 January 1972
How do you want to live? (H.M.S.O., 1972)
The Card-Players 6 May 1970
Encounter, October 1970
The Building 9 February 1972
New Statesman, 17 March 1972
Posterity 17 June 1968
New Statesman, 28 June 1968
Dublinesque 6 June 1970
Encounter, October 1970
Homage to a Government 10 January 1969
Sunday Times, 19 January 1969
This Be The Verse April? 1971
New Humanist, August 1971
How Distant 24 November 1965
Listener, 26 October 1971
Sad Steps 24 April 1968
New Statesman, 28 June 1968
Solar 4 November 1964
Queen, 25 May 1966
Annus Mirabilis 16 June 1967
Cover (Oxford), February 1968
Vers de Société 19 May 1971
New Statesman, 18 June 1971
Show Saturday 3 December 1973
Encounter, February 1974
Money 19 February 1973
Phoenix, Autum/Winter 1973–4
Cut Grass 3 June 1971
Listener, 29 July 1971

The Explosion   5 January 1970
    'Poem of the Month' broadside, 1970

UNCOLLECTED POEMS 1940–1972

Ultimatum   June? 1940
    Listener, 28 November 1940
Story
    Cherwell, 13 February 1941
A Writer
    Cherwell, 8 May 1941
May Weather
    Cherwell, 3 June 1941
Observation
    Oxford University Labour Club Bulletin,
    22 November 1941
Disintegration
    Oxford University Labour Club Bulletin,
    February 1942
Mythological Introduction
    Arabesque, Hilary term 1943
A Stone Church Damaged by a Bomb
    Oxford Poetry 1942–3, June 1943
Femmes Damnées   1943
    Sycamore Broadsheet 27, 1978
Plymouth   25 June 1945
    Mandrake, May 1946
Portrait   7 November 1945
    Mandrake, May 1946
The Dedicated   18 September 194•
    XX Poems
Modesties   13 May 1949
    XX Poems
Fiction and the Reading Public   25 February 1950
    Essays in Criticism, January 1954

Two Portraits of Sex: I – Oils   14 March 1950
   XX Poems (followed by 'II: Dry-Point':
   later 'Etching' 17 March 1950, which
   appeared by itself in *The Less Deceived*)
'Who called love conquering'   17 July 1950
   XX Poems
'Since the majority of me'   6 December 1950
   XX Poems
Arrival   1950
   XX Poems
Tops   29 October 1953
   Listen, Spring 1957
Success Story   11 March 1954
   The Grapevine (University of Durham),
   February 1957
Continuing to Live   22 April 1954
   A Keepsake for the New Library (SOAS), 1973
Pigeons   27 December 1955
   Departure, January 1957
Breadfruit   19 November 1961
   Critical Quarterly, Winter 1961
Love   7 December 1962
   Critical Quarterly, Summer 1966
'When the Russian tanks roll westward'   March? 1969
   Black Paper two: The Crisis in Education,
   1969
How   10 April 1970
   Wave, Autumn 1970
Heads in the Women's Ward   6 March 1972
   New Humanist, May 1972

UNCOLLECTED POEMS 1974–1984

The Life with a Hole in it   8 August 1974
   Poetry Book Society Supplement, Christmas
   1974

Bridge for the Living | December 1975
first performed at City Hall, Hull,
11 April 1981; *Poetry Book Society
Supplement*, Christmas 1981

Aubade | 29 November 1977
Times Literary Supplement, 23 December
1977

1952–1977 | 2 March 1978
Times Literary Supplement, 23 June 1978

'New eyes each year' | February 1979
Brynmor Jones Library, March 1979

The Mower | 12 June 1979
Humberside (Hull Literary Club
Magazine), Autumn 1979

'Dear CHARLES...'
Poems for Charles Causley, 1982

'By day, a lifted study-storehouse'
Brynmor Jones Library, October 1983

Party Politics
Poetry Review, January 1984

Index of titles

[213]

Index of first lines

[215]

[217]

expats p 105